TONY VENTRELLA

SMILE *in the*
MIRROR
Let Your Light Shine

Second Edition - Five New Chapters!

This book is about realizing how much power you actually have and how to use it

Tony Ventrella @ comcast.com

**POSITIVE ENERGY
PRODUCTIONS**

WWW.INFO@TYPEP.COM

SMILE *in the* MIRROR
Let Your Light Shine

By Tony Ventrella

Copyright © 2001 by Tony Ventrella

Library of Congress Control Number: 2002113348

SAN: 254-0835

ISBN 0-9714118-1-6

Edited by Linda Malnack and Tony Reineke, Authors' Advantage
tonireineke@attbi.com

Cover and text designed by Studio Pacific
www.studiopacific.com or call 206-935-8717

Distributed by Positive Energy Productions

Printed in the United States of America
By Sheridan Books

Third Edition

Ventrella Media Communications
www.VentrellaMC.Com
Email: Tony@VentrellaMC.Com
)

Acknowledgements

I want to thank my mother, who taught me the simple rules of life like "God is right there before you" and "Thy will be done." I had a happy childhood.

I thank my father, who made me learn haircutting, so I would know a trade and have something to be proud of early in life.

Thanks goes to my wife, Mika, for sticking by me through thick and thin (not that I've ever been thin). Her friendship, understanding and love have helped me through some sad times when I thought the light at the end of the tunnel was a freight train.

Thanks to Barbie Seifert, my publicist, whose constant support and sometimes annoying persistence made this book a reality.

Lastly, I want to thank everyone whose words, actions and lives have inspired this book, including small group of angels who remain close to me every day. Here is a poem dedicated to them.

My Angels in the Stars

Every night at midnight I gaze up at the sky
I read the face of heaven and breathe a little sigh.

I say hello to every star as they shine in all their glory,
For every sparkling light of night represents a story.

Of family and loved ones who've traveled far above,
Each shines for a different person and their never ending love.

Straight to the west my sister Bunny hovers in the sky.
Is that twinkling star I see the winking of her eye?

I crane my neck and look straight above. Is that Rose I see?
Her bright and happy star joined the others recently.

On a pitcher's mound in heaven Rick is in control.
It's been 20 years since that Indiana boy deeply touched my soul.

Off in the Southern sky I find a special star.
I've waited for you Jennifer to tell me where you are.

The one I talk to last each night is the brightest star I see.
My dad seems at home up there as he watches over me.

Ever since my childhood I wanted to study the stars.
The fantasy of my young life was to travel straight to Mars.

History books will tell you the stars are supposed to be
Guiding lights for ships at night for Mariners to see.

But I have a feeling as I look up there and study nature's show,
That every one of those brilliant stars offers a special glow.

In memory of someone who made the trip above,
To touch the face of heaven and fill the world with love.

To Mike,

Keep smiling!

CONTENTS

continued

CONTENTS

Introduction

SMILE IN THE MIRROR

Of all the things you wear, your expression is the most important.

—Unknown

I got up at 7:42 a.m. today. It was raining. I love that sound, so peaceful. It makes you want to go back to sleep. But I didn't. I looked out the window to confirm that it was really raining, walked into the bathroom, then stood in front of the mirror and smiled.

"Hi Tony. How are you today?" There I was smiling back at myself, saying hello.

What a pleasant man, I thought, always smiling, and he's talking to me.

You see, by smiling into the mirror and talking to yourself you do two things. First, you assure yourself that the first person you see in the morning will smile at you. Second, you see your own face smiling and at times during the day you can refer back to that moment if you need to.

The image of your own smiling face can help lift your spirits throughout the day.

By the way, if you expected some deep analysis of brain waves and extensive study of human behavioral patterns in this book, let me crush your hopes right off the bat.

This book is about waking up to the simple fact that you are in charge of your own life. You forecast your own future. You plan your own level of happiness, your own level of success, your own level of mental and physical health. You are in control of the quality and quantity of friends and relationships.

This book is about realizing how much power you actually have and how to use it.

When you walk into a dark room the first thing you do without even thinking is turn on a light. You even try to turn on that light when you know the power is out. It's habit.

Life is the same. When you walk into a room dark with despair you may need to be the light. It might be something you say, or just a simple smile to assure everyone else that the situation will get better.

But it all starts with that first smile in the mirror as soon as you get out of bed in the morning.

———

As I've said, I want to share some things about life, my life and the wonder of the simple things in everyone's lives. After all, the best things in life are free, with the possible exception of this book.

I have collected stories of people, places and memories that make life special for me. In sharing those stories, I hope you'll recall moments and people that have done the same for you.

Growing up in Connecticut in the 1950's, I had only one dream, to be the play-by-play voice of the New York Yankees. Mel Allen was my hero. "Going, Going, Gone," was my favorite quote. "How about that?" was a close second. If I could only do what Mel did for a living it would be better than heaven.

So I did. Well, I made believe I did. In the back yard of our little house in Wilton I would hit rocks into the woods with an old baseball bat. I called play by play of every hit. I played imaginary World Series. Always the Yankees against the Dodgers. The Yankees always won. "How about that?"

After high school, community college, and a short stint in the army, I worked in my dad's barber shop. More about that later.

I started in the newspaper business in 1963, went into radio eight years later and then television in 1977. Early life lessons from both parents helped me to appreciate every step of my climb up the ladder of life.

I have learned to see the joy in everything every day. Rain or shine, hot or cold, Monday or Friday, every day is special. I've learned that every day is a gift, and once I learned to open the package, life was truly a joy. I want to show you how to find that kind of joy too.

Chapter One
LETTING YOUR LIGHT SHINE

Every good gift and every perfect gift is from above. . . .

—James 1:17

"What are you grateful for?" my mother asked.

"The stuffing." I said, diving mouth first into my Thanksgiving dinner.

"That's not what I mean. I want you to think of all the things that have happened to you this year, good and bad. Say a prayer of thanks, then you can eat."

I quickly reeled off a few things I could remember, said a fast prayer, then started eating. As I tasted the tender white meat of another big Thanksgiving turkey and scooped up a fork full of fluffy mashed potatoes, I glanced around the table at my family. My brother Phil and his wife, Fran, were there, as well as my sister Mary Jane, Mother, Dad and a friend of Dad's we knew only as Mr. Abbott. He was in his late 70's then, a bachelor all his life. He would have spent Thanksgiving alone if Mom didn't invite him every year. Catching a little food in his white mustache, "Old Man Abbott" as we called him, kept the conversation lively with stories of people and events from his childhood.

After dinner my mom took an old fruit cake box down from the cupboard above the refrigerator. Seven years earlier in 1953 a customer in my dad's barber shop gave the cake as a Christmas gift. After eating a few pieces that first year we put the box away and forgot about it until the following Thanksgiving. When my mom opened the box a year later the cake was nothing more than a black square unsuitable for eating. So she threw away the cake and kept the box. That year a new tradition started. From then on, every Thanksgiving, a note went into the box signed by everyone at the dinner table. Now, more than 44 years later, the tradition continues.

"You better come home now, Mom is going to have heart surgery." My heart sank. They sounded so frantic, and I felt helpless. My immediate reaction was to say a prayer. In the prayer came the quote, "Let your light shine."

On Thanksgiving Day, 1960, I wrote the note in the box. I listed all the things I could remember that happened that year. The Pirates beat my beloved Yankees in the World Series. I stopped to think about a guy named Bill Mazeroski who was having a good Thanksgiving. That year, he hit the home run that broke my heart and beat the Yankees 10-9 at Forbes Field in Pittsburgh. Enough about that, I was getting depressed. I wrote about the election that happened three weeks earlier. John F. Kennedy beat Richard Nixon by the closest margin in American history.

Finally I listed everyone at the dinner table. And on the bottom of the page I wrote Mom's favorite "Let your light shine." We used to tease her about it. "What's it mean, Mom? Carry a flashlight around with you?" She would smile and say, "Just express love wherever you go, that's what 'Let your light shine' means."

————

Now, living in the Northwest, my wife Mika and I fly to Connecticut every year to join my family for Thanksgiving, by far my favorite holiday. There was an exception though. In 1994 we decided to skip the long flight and stay in Seattle. Then just a week before Thanksgiving I got a frantic call from my brother Phil, then another call from my sister Mary Jane.

"You better come home now, Mom is going to have heart surgery."

My heart sank. They sounded so frantic, and I felt helpless. My immediate reaction was to say a prayer. In the prayer came the quote, "Let your light shine."

The next morning Mika and I grabbed a TWA flight to New York City, then drove to New Haven and Yale Hospital. We went

* * * * * *

right up to my mother's room. She was in a two-bed room with a curtain in between. Her bed was empty. Oh, God, were we too late? Or had they rushed her down to surgery sooner than we thought? Then I heard a woman's voice behind the curtain.

"It's okay dear, they do these operations all the time. You'll be fine. I'll pray for you."

I realized the voice was my mother's. As I opened the curtain I saw her sitting with another older lady holding her hand.

"Mom," I said, "I'm no doctor, but I think you're supposed to be in bed."

"It's okay," my mother said, "This poor little old lady hasn't had many visitors, she's scheduled for an operation tomorrow, and she's very scared. I told her I would pray for her. I'm just letting my light shine."

My mom's new friend had her operation the next day. It was a success.

The night before my mom's operation—a "valve job," as she described it—I sat on her bed and held her hand.

"Mom," I said, "how are you really doing?"

She looked around her, smiled and said, "This is really pretty nice. It's the first time I haven't had to cook on Thanksgiving."

On the flight back home to Seattle I thought about my mom's situation. Here an 83-year-old woman faced the frightening prospect that she may or may not live through an operation. And instead of feeling sorry for herself she took the time to comfort someone else.

Matthew 5:16 says "Let your light shine before men that they may see your good works, and glorify your father which is in heaven."

This book is about "letting your light shine," enjoying more of your life and sharing the simple wonders you encounter every single day.

* * * * * *

Focus Your Light

Picture yourself as a tiny flashlight in a dark room. As soon as the light is turned on the darkness is gone. It's almost like it was never there.

When you walk into a room filled with despair, gloom, boredom, tension—in other words, darkness—switch on that little flashlight with a smile, a kind word and/or a positive comment about something you just saw or heard about. You'll be amazed at the effect your little "flashlight" gesture has on the rest of the people in the room.

* * * * * *

Chapter Two
POSITIVE SELF-TALK

We cannot direct the wind, but we can adjust the sails.

—Anonymous

Okay, be honest. How many of you talk to yourself regularly? How much of the conversation is aloud? When you do talk to yourself, do you answer? If the answer is "yes" to any of these questions, I like you already.

I talk to myself all the time. "Turn left here. Oops, you missed the turn. Now you're lost. Why can't you read a map? Come on, Tony, pay attention." And sometimes it's worse. "Boy, you're dumb. What's the matter with you? Can't you read?" That's when self-talk turns ugly. It's called negative self-talk and does nothing for your self-esteem or your mood.

Einstein said it takes eleven positive stimuli to offset one negative. Wow, no wonder there are so many depressed people in the world. Every time you look in the mirror and ask, "Why am I so short, so fat, so skinny, so bald?" you make yourself feel bad. Try this instead: Look in that mirror and proclaim, "Thank God for another day on this earth. Another chance to make myself better, help someone who needs it, make a new friend!"

When someone asks how you're doing, be bold. Tell them "I feel great and I think I'm going to feel even better soon."

Every time I begin to feel sorry for myself, I think of my friend Rick and the best single example of positive self-talk I've ever heard.

It was the summer of 1980. I was working for WANE TV, Channel 15, in Fort Wayne, Indiana. I received a call from a Little League mom inviting me to the District 10 Championship game. She told me about a pitcher named Rick who was going to be honored prior to the game. He wouldn't be playing due to illness, but he would be tossing out the first pitch. She thought it would make a good human interest story.

Beyond that I knew nothing. I drove the WANE TV van to the field and arrived about 30 minutes before the game. One team was warming up on the field, while the other team had a meeting in their dugout.

Each team wore white knit uniforms with different colored trim. The contrast against the deep green grass made for a wonderful small town scene. Volunteers were cooking hot dogs and selling popcorn and candy at two different booths behind home plate. It was a Little League scene I had witnessed hundreds of times before and never tired of, though I had no idea how memorable this day would be.

As I approached one of the dugouts, I saw Rick through the gate behind first base. He was sitting in a wheel chair with his bandaged right leg propped up. He was tall and slender with short blond hair and sparkling clear blue eyes.

"I'm Tony," I said, reaching out my right hand.

"I know. I watch Channel 15 every night," Rick said with a big smile. "What are you doing here?"

He pulled back the blanket, looked down at his right leg, which had been amputated just below the knee, looked back up at the doctor and I and said 'Gee, you left me a lot more than I expected!'

It was then that I realized no one had warned Rick what a celebrity he had become. I told him we were doing a story on the tournament and would like to get some video of his "first ball" ceremony for the 11 o'clock news. He was surprised but happy to do an interview.

At this point I still was unsure exactly why Rick was unable to play. I assumed he had banged up his knee. I was about to learn something about my own preparation and a certain 12-year-old boy's character.

* * * * * *

"How long do you think you'll be out of action?" I asked Rick, tilting the microphone toward him for his answer. "Out of action," he said with a smile, "I won't be coming back at all. I have cancer. They're going to amputate my leg."

I was stunned and embarrassed, but Rick put me at ease, continuing his answer. "I'm glad to be here to support my team, and I might try to play after the operation, but for this season I'm a spectator."

His friendly eyes and gentle smile told me something about his courage in the first two minutes of our conversation. I knew I wanted to get to know his family. We finished the interview and shot video of the ceremony. Rick threw out the first ball from the mound, smiled and waved to the crowd. My eyes filled with tears when the crowd of over a thousand parents, kids, Little League officials and players gave Rick a two-minute standing ovation.

As I sat and watched a couple innings of the game, I talked to some of the spectators about Rick. I found out his dad had been laid off from his job at Motorola the day before Rick was diagnosed with cancer. Later I met Rick's parents and they told me the operation to remove his leg would happen in two weeks. They also invited me to their home for cake and coffee whenever I was in town.

In the next two weeks I visited the family several times. They invited me to stop by again after Rick's operation. The morning after the surgery I knocked at the front door of their house, not knowing what to expect. Rick's mother was smiling when she answered the door. She invited me in and couldn't wait to tell me the news.

"Tony, do you know what Rick said, when he woke up after the operation? He pulled back the blanket, looked down at his right leg, which had been amputated just below the knee, looked back up at the doctor and I and said 'Gee, you left me a lot more than I expected!'"

That, my friends, is positive self-talk at its best.

* * * * * *

7

Bright Idea
Feed Your Brain

A. Abraham Lincoln said, "Most people are about as happy as they make up their minds to be." Your brain is a wonderful, natural computer with hundreds of times the potential. Feed your mind positive thoughts every day.

B. Be careful of the things you say when you talk to yourself. They will be reflected in your life style, in your dealings with others and in your eventual level of happiness.

C. Stand guard at the door of thought. Advertisers use the power of suggestion to sell us everything from bread to automobiles, painkillers to bug killers. It is their job to make you believe you need their product. They spend millions every year flooding the television and radio airwaves and print media with images and thoughts that touch all of our emotions. Soon we've talked ourselves into needing whatever product they're selling. The same is true with negative ideas, except in this case you are the advertiser and you are also the customer. If you talk negatively soon you'll begin to think that way too.

D. Be a child again. Have you ever noticed that whenever it snows most adults get all upset. "Oh no, this will really mess up my schedule." Or "I hate driving in this stuff. It's not that I don't know how; it's all those other people who don't." Now observe most little kids say when it snows: "Wow! Is there enough to build a snowman? Where can we go sledding? Is school closed today?"

* * * * * *

Chapter Three
NEW YEAR RESOLUTIONS

People with goals succeed because they know where they're going.

—Earl Nightingale

Let's face it, a new year is an opportunity to do what we really meant to do last year. Lose that weight, save that money, fix that gutter, write that apology, watch television every night. Never mind, we did that one.

The list of excuses can be impressive. I didn't have time, the economy wasn't right, I was too tired, had no support, the boss wouldn't let me, it was raining, it was too hot, too cold, too dark, too bad.

Let's get to the real reason. We didn't want to do it badly enough. If we had really wanted to, we would have found a way. The wonderful thing about being human is that we always find a way to do what we want to do. It's just that some people take longer.

Isn't it true that our minds work miracles when we see something we really want? We always seem to figure out a way to get it. For example, imagine there is a million dollars cash waiting for you in a mailbox in Spokane. All you have to do is get there. You start driving from Seattle. Twenty miles east on I-90 you get a flat tire. Are you going to quit there, give up, make an excuse? I don't think so. You'll change that tire and continue on. A few miles east in Ellensburg your car overheats. The mechanic says, "Forget it, this car will never run again." Will you quit now? Just forget the million bucks because the car overheated? Or will you find a way to get there without a car? You will. You'll walk if you have to.

Obviously, the million dollars creates an incentive that jogging doesn't. That's where your creative mind needs to come in. Jogging three times a week will lead to more energy, better sleep, fewer illnesses and better fitting clothes. Once you create a new image of yourself in your mind, the actual task will not seem as difficult. Be sure to keep your eyes on the "goal."

Okay, let's get to it, goal setting in seven easy steps. I only said "easy" so you'd keep reading. It really isn't that easy, but the results are worth the effort.

Focus Your Light

Step One: Get a long yellow legal pad. Get your favorite pen, not a pencil. We need to commit here. Write down everything you've ever wanted to do in your entire life. No kidding. I mean everything. The big plans, the small plans, practical, wild and crazy, everything. Try not to forget all the financial, personal, spiritual, physical, and material aspects. Write them all down, and leave a little space after each one. Don't put them into categories yet, just think and write as fast as you can. If you want to save more money, how much? If you want to invest more, how much? Do you want to pay off your credit cards, lose 10 pounds, walk your dog more, be nicer to your mother-in-law? Or walk your mother-in-law and be nicer to your dog? It's your choice.

Next, on a separate sheet of paper make a material list. This is fun. What "things" do you want? It's okay to want things, as long as you write it down—a new car, a stereo, a leather coat. Go ahead, dream and imagine, and continue writing. The key element in listing your goals is to believe you can have them all. Let your imagination run wild. Ask yourself, what would I want if I knew I could have it? That will really set your mind free.

Step Two: Look at every item separately. Under each item ask yourself why it's on the list. Why do I want this or that? What is the real reason? If you are unable to think of a reason, the goal will never come to fruition. For example, "I'm going to Spokane because there's a million dollars waiting in a mailbox for me." Every time you want

*Set a deadline.
You won't reach your
goals unless there are
deadlines.*

to quit, the reason will come back and inspire you to keep going.

Step Three: In the left-hand column place a number one next to any goal you hope to achieve in one year. Do the same with your long-term goals. Write down a "3" for three years, a "5" for five years, and so on.

Step Four: Take all the goals with ones next to them and begin a separate list on a different sheet of paper. Under each goal write a sentence describing how it will feel once you've achieved that specific goal. Feel the emotions that will come from achieving that goal. See yourself 10 pounds lighter. Enjoy the feeling. See your bank account with two thousand more dollars in it. Enjoy the feeling. Do that with all your goals, especially those you want to work on immediately.

Step Five: Make a list of all the information you need to know to start toward your goal. For example, to start a savings plan pay a quick visit to your bank to meet with a financial advisor. Or perhaps it's time to join a gym if your goal is weight loss and better health.

Step Six: List any people you know who might have information that can help you toward your goal. Get on the phone immediately and call one of them. Don't put it off. You'll feel like you're already making progress because you are.

Step Seven: Set a deadline. You won't reach your goals unless there are deadlines. "I will lose ten pounds and weigh 135 pounds by April 15th of this year." "I will save one hundred dollars every month this year." Be specific, and reward the small victories.

Have fun setting goals. It will make a tremendous difference in your life. Start now, don't look back and, most important of all, never give up!

* * * * * *

Chapter Four
MY FAVORITE SPORT

Thank you, God, for this good life and forgive us if we do not love it enough.

—Garrison Keillor

I was speaking to a class full of fifth graders when one of them asked, "What's your favorite sport?"

"Living," I said. Everyone laughed.

I explained, "Living is the one thing I enjoy doing more than anything else. Every part of living. Getting up in the morning is a joy because it means I have another shot at life. Another chance to be better than yesterday, another chance to meet new people, help change the life of someone in need, smell a flower, eat my favorite kind of bagel."

There is so much joy in life that it amazes me when people can't see it. In my profession I've met athletes whose salary is well into the millions, but they still find themselves trapped in the material world, the world of bigger cars, bigger houses, bigger alarm systems. My years of covering professional sports and athletes have been enjoyable, but recently tainted by the attitudes of some I come into contact with. To be good enough to play Major League baseball would be a joy, a wonderful privilege. I'm sure many players know that, but I'm certain many don't take the time to appreciate their special gifts.

I think we should all slow down a little bit and appreciate what we have. Not just the things we possess, but all of the wonderful intangible items we take for granted.

In a recent snow storm, power at our house was lost for three days. When those lights came back on I had to smile and admit I take so much for granted.

Look at our supermarkets, every shelf overflowing with fresh produce, meats, fish, chicken, frozen foods, wonderful breads and cakes.

Look around you during the next snowstorm. Before you curse the slippery roads or the driver in front of you, stop to take in the beauty of nature. In Robert Frost's poem, "Stopping by Woods on a Snowy Evening," the poet gives us a lesson in appreciating life.

Whose woods these are I think I know.
His house is in the village though;
He will not see me stopping here
To watch his woods fill up with snow.

My little horse must think it queer
To stop without a farmhouse near
Between the woods and frozen lake,
The darkest evening of the year.

He gives his harness bells a shake
To ask if there is some mistake.
The only other sound's the sweep
Of easy wind and downy flake.

The woods are lovely, dark and deep,
But I have promises to keep,
And miles to go before I sleep,
And miles to go before I sleep.

* * * * * *

In December of 1995, the New England states had plenty of snow to appreciate. As I watched a CNN weather report about cars sliding into each other and frozen power lines, I began to worry about my 84-year-old parents living in Connecticut. I phoned my mother.

"Mom how are you guys getting along with all that snow?"

She paused for a moment, then said, "I just look outside across the back yard; it is so beautiful."

Every spring when the ground thawed in New England my father would plant his garden. It was always impressive. He had tomatoes, lettuce, several fruit trees, rhubarb, squash, string beans and corn. A visit to my parents' house always included a garden tour. With a true sense of pride my dad showed off his harvest every year. At the end of the summer he gave most of the food away. "We'll never eat it all, might as well give to some of these families with kids," he said. Working a garden is a terrific way to appreciate life.

Focus Your Light

Make a list of all the things you appreciate in this wonderful life. Clean water coming out of the tap. Your favorite TV shows. Working on your car. Shopping at the mall. Meeting that special friend for a cup of coffee.

If you really want to appreciate life, keep the list out all the time and add to it every day. I put my list on the refrigerator with one of those little magnets. In fact, those little magnets are one of the things I appreciate. I have dozens of them. Did I mention rubber stamps? Another chapter maybe.

Chapter Five
PERFECT MOMENTS

It takes so little to make people happy. Just a touch, if we know how to give it, just a word fitly spoken, a slight readjustment of some bolt or pin or bearing in the delicate machinery of a soul.

—Frank Crane

My sister Mary Jane called today. No big news. Nobody got married or divorced, nobody's sick and nobody died. It was a nice day and she wanted to share that with me. In fact, it was not only a nice day, it was a perfect day. She lives in Connecticut where perfect days often happen in autumn and spring, not so often in the summer.

This summer day, though, was perfect. Mary Jane told me it hadn't rained in weeks, the temperature was in the mid-70s, humidity was low, she felt great and there was a free concert in town that night.

You see, it shouldn't take much to be a perfect day. There is so much beauty around us already we just need to see it to realize that most days are nearly perfect. I sense I may be losing you now. You think I'm sniffing glue, don't you? Sorry, I've never liked glue, except for the stuff we used in third grade. But I didn't sniff that; I ate it.

I choose to see the beauty in simple things. I call them perfect moments and I make a mental note of them every time they happen. Every year I go to the Red Barn Tree Farm in Sumner, Washington, to get my Christmas tree. That's a perfect moment. As soon as I catch the scent of a Christmas tree, all kinds of great memories come back to me.

In real life, perfect moments are so much better than that. You don't have to be handsome or beautiful to have a perfect moment. You need not be skinny or muscular. All you need to do is appreciate all the beauty that exists in your life. Look for it, enjoy it, remember it.

One Saturday morning in 1982 in a little town called Moscow, Idaho, I woke up early to go for a run. I was in Eastern Washington to cover the Apple Cup football game between the University of Washington and Washington State University.

I stepped out my door at 7:00 a.m. greeted by the cold, biting morning air. A two-inch snowfall had covered the rolling hills of the Palouse with a fluffy blanket of white the evening before. My run was easy and smooth, and I was overwhelmed by the beauty of the morning. It was a perfect moment.

I got back to the hotel in time to join the rest of the crew for breakfast. Two of them complained of hangovers from their activities the night before. They were unable to tune in to the beauty around them and because of that missed a perfect moment.

Two years ago my wife and I spent a week in New England in October. Our first stop was Cooperstown, New York, and the Baseball Hall of Fame. Halfway through our five-hour drive to Cooperstown, we stopped in a little diner south of Troy, New York, on Route 22. We ordered eggs and hash browns and toast. A little fat, a little cholesterol, but another perfect moment.

During the next few days we strolled the quaint streets of Cooperstown and toured the Hall of Fame and Doubleday Field. Then we drove across New York to Vermont and stopped at the Norman Rockwell Museum in Arlington. We had lots of perfect moments that week and we'll always remember them.

* * * * * *

Sit down with a pad and pen tonight and write down all of your perfect moments. Too bad perfect moments on television include alcohol and all the "beautiful people." In real life, perfect moments are so much better than that. You don't have to be handsome or beautiful to have a perfect moment. You need not be skinny or muscular. All you need to do is appreciate all the beauty that exists in your life. Look for it, enjoy it, remember it.

———

I'm glad my sister called. I'm glad she went to a free band concert on a perfect summer night in Connecticut. It reminded me that perfect moments happen every day of our lives. We just need to slow down long enough to see them.

Bright Idea
Make the Most of Your Time

A. Here's an eye-opening thought. Or maybe we should call it an eye-closing thought. We're going to be dead a lot longer than we're alive. So why not treat every day as the treasure it is? Be grateful for every day and make the best of it.

B. Get up 15 minutes earlier than you usually do. That buys you an hour and 45 minutes of extra time every week. That's almost two extra days a month, over twenty more days per year. That was easy, wasn't it?

C. In the first five minutes of your extra time each day pinpoint two things for which you are grateful and enjoy those thoughts for a full minute each. Then take another minute to ask yourself, "How can I do better in every way today than I did yesterday?" In the final two minutes of your "quiet time," let all the energy you need flow into your body through your mind. Now you are ready for the day.

* * * * * *

D. Avoid time wasters. Make a list before you go to the store. At night before you go to sleep, make a list of the six most important things you have to do tomorrow and do the first one as soon as possible when you get up.

E. Remember to live now, love now, say "I care about you" now, say "I'm sorry" now. "Yesterday is a canceled check; tomorrow is a promissory note; today is the only cash you have—so spend it wisely" (Kay Lyons).

Chapter Six

MOTHER'S DAY

The best portion of a good life is the little nameless, unremembered acts of kindness and of love.

—William Wordsworth

What are you getting for your mom for Mother's Day? Have you thought about it? Flowers, candy? Maybe you'll take her out to brunch or dinner. Or maybe she'll cook for everyone else like my mom did for so many years.

Want to know what I'm getting for my mom? A list. That's right, a list. I'm making a list of everything my mother has done for me in my life. A sort of thank you card. It's going to take a while. I could write a book. In fact, I did. I'm going all the way back to my birth, trying to recall everything she ever did to make my life easier then and better now.

First on the list is the day I met her, the day I was born. It was 4 o'clock in the morning on June 18, 1944 in Norwalk, Connecticut. We didn't say much to each other. I slept all day and she smiled a lot. The next day I cried and she smiled a lot. It was the beginning of a wonderful relationship. She always made me feel safe.

I had my share of childhood ailments. I remember chicken pox. She explained that it would go away in a couple of days and it did. I asked her why chickens didn't get it. She laughed. She always made me feel smart and funny.

March 12, 1956 was a very sad day in my family. My sister Bunny died that day. Three days later at the funeral it was Mom who comforted everybody. She told me to always remember Bunny and celebrate her life as part of my own. She taught me how to live my life to the fullest.

It was mom who went to Grandpa Ventrella's house and sat with him during his final moments. No one could go into the room without crying. Grandpa kept telling everyone, "Take me home, take me home." No one understood what he meant. My mother calmly took his hand and said "I'll take you home, Pa." A few minutes later he died. My mom always knew what to say and when to say it. She taught me about grace under pressure.

> *"Take me home, take me home." No one understood what he meant. My mother calmly took his hand and said "I'll take you home, Pa."*

Every day when I came home from school my mom would be there. She'd open her arms and say, "My son is home, my son is home." She always made me feel important.

I watched my mom work side by side next to Dad in his barber shop for years when the family needed money to pay my sister's hospital bills. She taught me how to be responsible.

Every day, as long as I can remember, Mom has read her Bible and *Science and Health with Key to the Scriptures* by Mary Baker Eddy. She taught me how to have faith in all circumstances.

Focus Your Light

On Mother's Day this year when you get ready to send flowers or candy or take Mom to lunch remember the list. Take the time to write out all the things she has done for you over the years. All the flowers and candy in the world can't beat that.

* * * * * *

Me, age 10

My 1962 Wilton High
School graduation
picture

Dad, Mr Abbott, and me
Thanksgiving 1964

Me, sister Mary Jane, Dad, and Mom.
Reading from the "Memory Box" Thanksgiving 1994

Sister-in-law Fran, Dad, Mom, Mika,
sister Mary Jane
Thanksgiving 1997

Me and Rick - 1980
Ft. Wayne, IN

Rick - 1980

Dad in his garden
Danbury, CT

Sister Mary Jane and Me
1997

Me, Mom, Bunny
1953

My sister Bunny - 1953

Me and Bunny
1954

Me, Mary Jane,
Bunny 1954

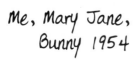

Uncle Ralph interviewing Johnny Podres
from the Dodgers for WWSC Radio - 1955

Johnnie Corr, Highschool Football Picture- 1961

Willie Mays

Mickey Mantle

Dave Appelbaum on graduation day
Williams College, Williamstown, MA
June 1964

Aunt Rita, me, and Uncle Ralph
Florida-2001

Dad's barber shop,
Norwalk, CT
June 1956

Getting a
haircut from
Dad - 1987

Me cutting a
friend's hair
1962

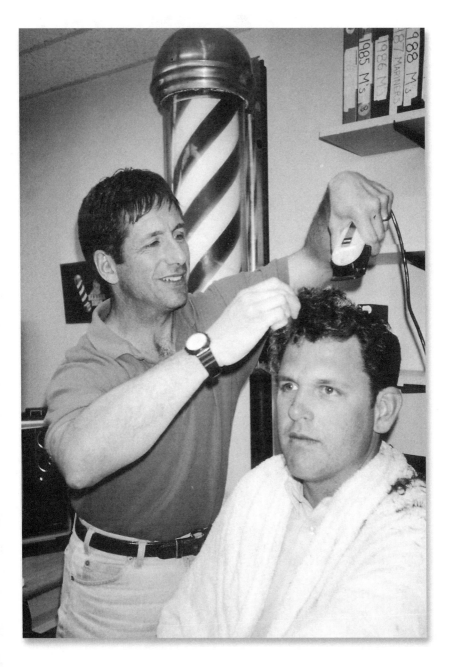

Giving a haircut to KING 5 "customer" Bill Rockey

Dad in the navy
1928

Dad going fishing
1998

Grandpa Romano,
Uncle Ralph,
Grandma Romano,
Rutland, VT - 1960

Chapter Seven

"HERE'S MY NEPHEW WITH SPORTS"

Laughter is not at all a bad beginning for a friendship and it is by far the best ending for one.

—Oscar Wilde

The radio station had a certain smell to it. I think it was a combination of the old tube-driven equipment, cigarette smoke, typewriter ribbon, the cologne of one of the newsmen and pots of coffee heated a few minutes past their prime. That smell was the first impression of my first radio station experience. It was the summer of 1955 in Glens Falls, New York, at WWSC Radio. Uncle Ralph, my mother's brother, worked there. He was in his prime as a radio sportscaster doing a show called the "Pepsi Cola Sports Parade."

Uncle Ralph's road to success in the broadcasting business wasn't by the usual route. As a baby, he was given eye drops in the hospital, but a horrible mistake in the solution cost him the sight in one eye.

Then while serving in the army during World War II, Uncle Ralph suffered a head injury leading to seizures that would bother him for the next 20 years. He spent 10 years in a Veterans Hospital as doctors tried to find a solution to the seizures. While in the hospital, Uncle Ralph took an aptitude test in an attempt to find a suitable career. He tested strong in the field of broadcasting and with the help of a GI loan attended the Leland Powers School of Broadcasting in Boston.

Uncle Ralph took his first job at the Glens Falls radio station on June 1, 1953. Now two years later I traveled to upstate New York with my dad and mom.

After Uncle Ralph introduced me to some of the staff at WWSC he handed me a piece of paper with three baseball scores on it. He told me to go into the studio, sit at the table with the microphone mounted on it and practice reading the scores. As a 10-year-old, I just thought he wanted me to practice my reading. Then all of a sudden in the middle of his own hourly sportscast I heard Uncle Ralph say, "And here's my nephew with the scores." I was stunned for a second. Then I read the scores as well as any other 10-year-old could've done. Were the jobs of Mel Allen, Win Elliott and Les Keiter in jeopardy? I don't think so.

Always look at the lighter side of life and help others do the same. And enjoy the heck out of every day because, in his own words, "Life's too short."

I didn't have time to be nervous. That doesn't mean I was good. I just didn't have time to be nervous. When I was finished several people at the station clapped their hands. I was embarrassed, but I knew at that moment what I wanted to do for a living. Uncle Ralph, the one-eyed man with all the jokes, had opened the door and I was ready to run through.

Right after Uncle Ralph got his job in Glens Falls, New York, he started a bowling league for blind people. He and 52 others were part of the first Blind Bowling Club in America. In fact, he helped create the "Bowling Rail" that blind bowlers hold on to while they roll the ball down the lane. Uncle Ralph is always doing something for others.

Now Uncle Ralph is nearing his 80s and lives in Florida with his wife Rita. Ralph doesn't do radio anymore, but he still tells jokes, lots of them. He works small dinners, large banquets, luncheons, trade shows, birthdays and weddings. He tells jokes, makes people

* * * * * *

laugh and never charges a dime for his work. The charming 5'5" white-haired Italian man with one glass eye has done over 3,500 benefit performances. Any time he gets a call from a Veterans Hospital his answer is "yes."

The most important thing he does is make people laugh...for free. In fact, I'll prove it to you. Here are five of Uncle Ralph's jokes. They've been told thousands of times each to thousands of people, most of them over 65 who feel much younger thanks to the laughter provided by my Uncle Ralph.

Uncle Ralph's Jokes

Ma: What's a yet?
Pa: What do you mean?"
Ma: "Says in the paper, a woman shot herself and the bullet is in her yet."

Theater manager: "If the baby cries, you must leave and I'll return your money."
Man: Halfway through the movie, "You like the movie?"
Wife: "It stinks, pinch the baby."

Man: "I did exactly what the sign says and I got arrested."
Wife: "What did the sign say?"
Man: "Men's room, use the stairs."

Worker: "Lady, your husband was run over by a steam roller."
Lady: "Slide him under the door, I'm not dressed."

From Uncle Ralph I learned two things: Always look at the lighter side of life and help others do the same. And enjoy the heck out of every day because, in his own words, "Life's too short."

* * * * *

Bright Idea
Laugh, Laugh, Laugh

A. Read or watch something funny right before you go to sleep every night.

B. When my mom was in the hospital for surgery we made a point of sitting around her bed and laughing and joking about family matters. We all felt better. Even Mom's doctor said her quick recovery was a direct result of the laughter.

C. Laugh with your children. Let them laugh at you. My kids derive hearty laughter from my choice of music and clothes. Frankly, I see nothing wrong with my rugby shirts and Perry Como CDs.

D. Use that smile. Your face has over 80 muscles that get a little workout every time you smile. I've been smiling all my life. I have one of the strongest faces on earth.

Chapter Eight

THE BIG DEAL

When you part from your friend, you grieve not. For that which you love most in him may be clearer in his absence, as the mountain to the climber is clearer from the plain.

—Kahlil Gibran

It was the summer of 1955. The Dodgers were still in Brooklyn. Hard core Dodger fans still showed up at Ebbets Field on Flatbush Avenue hoping for something they had never seen, a World Series Championship. Let me make one thing clear, though, I was a Yankee fan. I thought the Yankees were still the best team in baseball, even if they'd won 104 games the previous year and still finished seven games behind the Cleveland Indians. Cleveland got stomped in four straight by the Giants anyway.

My best friend that year was a kid named Johnnie Corr, a tall blond kid who seemed to be good at every sport and popular with every kid in school. He also had a nice baseball card collection and the one card I wanted: 1953 Mickey Mantle.

With two days to go before the end of the school year we made plans for "The Big Deal." We would meet at my house on Newsome Lane in Wilton at 12 noon the day after school got out for the summer.

I got up early that morning. I didn't have to—it was summer—but I was excited about the deal. Johnnie's mom dropped him off at the end of our driveway at noon on the button. It was a warm day, but I still had on the Yankee jacket Aunt Jane had given me. She lived in Scarsdale and had season tickets to Yankee Stadium. Johnnie was dressed in a tee-shirt, jeans, baseball cap and sneakers.

He had a shoe box filled with baseball cards, an impressive collection that included such greats as Yogi Berra and Phil Rizzuto of the Yankees; Dusty Rhodes and Bobby Thompson of the Giants; and Duke Snider,

Pee Wee Reese and Roy Campanella of the Dodgers. Those cards were impressive all right, but it was the "Mick" I wanted. And I had the card Johnnie wanted, a 1954 Willie Mays. In fact, I was firmly in the driver's seat because I had *two* Willie Mays cards.

The deal happened at about 12:10 p.m. Johnnie handed me the Mickey Mantle at the same time I handed him Willie Mays. We both smiled, our day complete, maybe our summer.

Johnnie and I spent the rest of the day playing Wiffle® Ball, a game that allowed even an ordinary kid like me to throw a curve ball. His mom came to pick him up at 4 o'clock. Our memorable day was over. We would see each other in the halls of Wilton Junior High and at high school for the next six years.

I live my life the way he would have lived his. Lots of laughter, never taking myself too seriously, always trying to appreciate the simple things in life. Like baseball caps, comfortable sneakers and the ability to strike out anybody with a Wiffle® ball.

After high school Johnnie went away to the University of Bridgeport where he starred as quarterback for the football team. One summer evening I was jogging at the old Wilton High School track when Johnnie stopped by. We joked and laughed and even remembered "The Big Deal" from years earlier.

"I'm leaving, Tony," Johnnie said, "and I just wanted to say goodbye. I'm joining the Marines."

That was the last time I saw Johnnie. On December 28, 1968, 13 years after the most memorable day of my childhood, Lt. John Corr was killed in action in Vietnam. I was home on lunch break from my job at my dad's barber shop when I heard the news. My eyes filled with tears as they had five years earlier when President John F. Kennedy was killed, but Johnnie Corr dying 10,000 miles from home cut out a piece of my heart.

* * * * * *

Since that sad day 30 years ago, I have sold my baseball cards. It doesn't matter that my 1953 Mickey Mantle would be worth over $3,000 today. What does matter is that the memory of Johnnie Corr lives on.

I live my life the way he would have lived his. Lots of laughter, never taking myself too seriously, always trying to appreciate the simple things in life. Like baseball caps, comfortable sneakers and the ability to strike out anybody with a Wiffle® ball.

In this age of e-mail, voice mail, and pagers that wake you in the night, when the number two killer of young people in this country is hand guns and the lure of material gain drives normal people to strike out against each other, something has to be done.

The answer isn't that complicated. The government can't do it; we must do it ourselves. We simply have to regain our perspective and tell ourselves what's really important.

For me, it's memories of the good times, the good people like Johnnie Corr and the good days like that day in June long ago when we traded Mickey Mantle for Willie Mays.

Focus Your Light

A wonderful speaker and author, Zig Ziglar, once said, "You can have everything in life you want if you will just help enough other people get what they want." Every good and fair businessperson will tell you to "leave something on the table." In every deal, always make it a double-win situation by giving a little and taking a little.

* * * * *

Chapter Nine
THE SUMMER OF '57

To be able to enjoy one's past life is to live twice.

—James Montgomery

Summertime. I've been out of school 40 years and I still look forward to the summer. So many memories to look back on, so many adventures to look forward to.

In the summer of 1957 I lived in Wilton, Connecticut. I had just passed 7th grade, no small task considering my study habits. If only Yankee Statistics had been a class, I would have gotten an "A."

My summer adventures started on the last day of school. I had the same bus driver all year and it seemed at least once a week he'd talk about his Harley-Davidson motorcycle. Finally, on the last day of school he offered me a ride, so I skipped my bus stop and had him drive me all the way to the bus barn at the end of the route. The he let me hop on the back of his bike and I got a ride home on the Harley. My parents wouldn't have approved, but they weren't home when we got there and until now my "Harley ride home" has remained a secret.

The Fourth of July was memorable that year. My best friend was Dave Appelbaum. His dad was a doctor and set off the fireworks every summer right out in front of his house. Dave and I chugged Kool-Aid, played Wiffle® Ball and waited for darkness when the show would begin. First came the small stuff, sparklers and the little ones that spin and whistle, then the bigger ones that light up the sky and make everyone cover their ears. After the blast we roasted marshmallows. Nothing in the world is less nutritional and more fun than a roasted marshmallow.

In the summer of '57 we had yellow jackets, lots of them. They had nested in the ground and were waiting for unsuspecting people with rotary mowers to get them all riled up. My dad had a solution to the problem. A kerosene-soaked rag would do the trick. Light the rag on fire and burn them out.

One day when Dad was working at the barber shop my best friend Dave Appelbaum and I were playing Wiffle® Ball in my front yard and noticed a few yellow jackets circling a hole in the ground near one of the flower beds.

I remembered the soaked rag trick. One problem though...we couldn't find any kerosene. So we used gasoline. And we didn't bother to soak the rag...we just poured the gas into the hole and threw a match in. Fascinated by the intensity of the explosion, we did it over and over again. Only a call to my dad by a disturbed Mr. Wargo across the street put an end to our fun.

The bees had the last word though. In 1998, on a visit to my parent's house, I was working in the yard with Dad, using the weedeater around a flower bed, when a dozen yellow jackets paid me back for blowing their ancestors to smitherines. It all evens out I guess.

———

Back to the summer of '57.

One day a week Dave and I got to go to his father's downtown office in Norwalk. It was three blocks away from Herman's Smoke Shop. We didn't smoke, but Herman had the biggest selection of baseball cards in the city. The balding roly-poly Herman was nice to us, even though we didn't spend much money.

"Hey boys," he told us, "look for the packs with the little stars on back. Those are the best cards." He was right, and we became customers for life, though I still don't smoke.

As the summer of '57 drew to a close, the most important event occurred. I kissed Barbara Koenig right on the lips. It was the most exciting moment of my life. We were at the Norwalk Theatre. The movie cost 75 cents, popcorn was about a quarter, the kiss was free, but boy did I have to work for it. It took me half an hour just to put my arm around her. Then I couldn't figure out what to do with my hand. The kiss itself was almost accidental. For a fleeting moment we turned toward each other and it happened.

When the movie ended my parents picked us up and drove Barbara home. There was no way I would try to kiss her again. I just shook hands with her and floated back to my car. To this day I have no memory of the movie, just the kiss.

As I sat in my 8th grade classes that September wondering how the Yankees would do in the pennant race, my mind wandered back to the summer. The secret motorcycle ride, fireworks in the Appelbaum's front yard, blowing up yellow jackets, Herman's Smoke Shop and the magic moment at the Norwalk Theater with Barbara Koenig.

Focus Your Light

Memories are wonderful, but only because the emotions created by those memories help shape decisions for the future. I decorate my Christmas tree the same way every year because of memories. I eat ice cream on hot days because of memories. I don't put my tongue on the ice tray in the freezer anymore because of memories. See what I mean.

Chapter Ten

ONE BARBER, NO WAITING

A man without a smiling face must not open a shop.

—Chinese Proverb

Although I've been in sports journalism for 30 years, my career began next to a barber chair. I worked for my dad at Ventrella's Barber Shop on Main Street in Norwalk, Connecticut, from 1961 until 1967.

My dad knew only one business, the barber business. He opened his own shop in 1928, at the age of 16. When most young men were struggling through high school my dad was running his own business.

Dad thought it would be nice if I would learn the trade too. In fact, he made me learn the trade. I was in 9th grade at Wilton Junior High School when I first picked up the barber scissors. My dad made me practice bringing the scissors and comb in an upward motion, making sure never to let the scissors slide off the comb and directly into the hair on the imaginary head of the imaginary person sitting in my imaginary barber chair. I practiced for one hour a day for six months until I had the scissors-comb motion down pat. That's when the "real" haircuts began.

"Hi! This is Tony Ventrella. How are you? I have a deal for you. Bring your kids to my shop at 6 p.m. and I'll cut their hair free. All you have to do is let my son, Tony, practice on them."

Can you imagine the fear in the hearts of some of those kids? It didn't matter though. The appeal of "free" haircuts with the promise that Dad would fix up my mistakes brought a steady flow of "practice heads" into the shop after hours.

Little by little, I learned to take equal amounts of hair off the left and right sides, even up the sideburns and trim the hair on top evenly all over. Tapering the back with scissors and comb was my specialty. Why not? I'd practiced for six months on the wall in the garage!

Within six months I was good enough to cut someone's hair without offering them a hat to cover it up. Dad had to fix up most of my "victims" at first, but soon he was able to just stand by and watch. By the beginning of 10th grade I was a pretty good barber for a 15-year-old kid. And I could do a "regular" haircut in seven minutes. My dad was a stickler for speed, and that's why my brother Phil came up with the motto, "One Barber, No Waiting."

Dad paid me $25 a week for working every day after school and all day Saturday. After a while he left me in charge, leaving early on a Saturday to go hunting for the weekend. To ensure I wouldn't close the shop early, he offered to let me keep all the money I took in the final hour every day. One night I kept the shop open until 7 p.m. and picked up an extra 15 bucks, a tidy sum when your entire week's pay is only $25.

> *To ensure I wouldn't close the shop early, he offered to let me keep all the money I took in the final hour every day.*

The lessons I learned working in the barber shop were invaluable. Sure I could cut hair, trim beards, even do a shave if needed, but, more important than that, I learned about people.

We had a part-time barber working the third chair named John Marino. At age 65 he had come to my dad and asked for work. He didn't need the money, just wanted something to do, having been forced to retire from his job due to his age. John stood 5'1" on his tiptoes and wore thick glasses. He wasn't a very good barber, but Dad gave him a job anyway.

"You'll never find a nicer person than John," my dad told me. "Watch how polite he is to the customers."

* * * * * *

Day after day I watched John help people with their coats, fuss with their haircuts, play with their children and generally make people smile.

Dad paid John $65 a week and every Saturday night with tears in his eyes John would try to give the money back. "You gave me a job. I am so grateful," John would say, "Here, keep the money." Dad would smile and tell him to go home.

On Sundays when most barbers enjoyed a much deserved day off, John would walk from his house to the hospital and cut hair for bedridden patients. He was that kind of man, always giving, always smiling.

John's life ended one cold and snowy New Year's morning. While walking down "hospital hill," John was struck by a car and killed. The driver was drunk.

John was survived only by his daughter. At the funeral my dad held her hand and told her how much people liked John, how his smile made people feel good. Through her tears, she managed a smile.

To this day, old-fashioned barber shops bring back memories. One time late on a winter afternoon I was alone in the shop getting ready to close. A man walked in dressed all in black. Maybe it was something I'd been reading before he came in, but for some reason I was convinced he was going to hold up the place.

All during his haircut he said nothing, just stared at me in the mirror. By the time he stood up to pay me, I had already decided to give him all the money in the register and explain it to my dad later.

He reached quickly into his black coat, and I knew he was going for his gun. Would my life end here in the barber shop? Would my bullet-riddled body show up in a photo on the front page of the newspaper? Well, apparently not. The quick move to his inside jacket pocket produced nothing more dangerous than his wallet. He paid and even gave me a tip. I didn't have much breath left to thank him with; only a high-pitched squeak came out. He must have thought

I reached puberty right at that moment. My voice had been normal throughout the entire haircut and now suddenly I was Donald Duck in a barber coat. He gave me a strange look, turned and walked out into the darkness.

"So, what's a quiet guy like you going to do for fun this weekend?" He looked at me in the mirror and without changing his expression he said, "I'm going to bury my wife today. She died Wednesday."

Making conversation with the customers was difficult for me in the beginning. I never knew what to say. It took me a couple of years to get up enough nerve to actually have an intelligent conversation with people whose ears and bald spots I was touching. One day, though, when I was well settled into my comfort zone of small talk, it backfired on me. Early on a Saturday morning a man walked in and sat down in my chair. He was my first customer of the day. I noticed he wasn't talking much and sat staring straight ahead as I cut his hair. Being the snappy conversationalist, I jumped right in with a cheerful and clever ice breaker. "So, what's a quiet guy like you going to do for fun this weekend?"

He looked at me in the mirror and without changing his expression he said, "I'm going to bury my wife today. She died Wednesday."

Meekly I replied, "I'm sorry," and finished the haircut without another word.

I never wanted to learn to be a barber, but now I'm glad for the ability to obtain a job in any state, hold a conversation with anyone and, most of all, spot a stick-up man from a mile away.

* * * * * *

Bright Idea
Get Along With Others

A. Dr. Martin Luther King, Jr. said, "We all came here on different ships, but we're in the same boat now." Be color blind. When you meet someone new look past their clothes and skin and into their soul. Look past their car and their house and their money or lack of same. Look right into their hearts.

B. Listen to your family, friends and co-workers. Really listen, then respond. Don't just wait for your turn to talk.

C. Don't gossip or complain. It's really boring for people around you and eventually brings your own attitude down too.

D. Know your neighbors, know their children and be nice to their pets. Talk about tolerance, love and compassion to your own kids and practice those qualities every day.

E. Practice random acts of kindness.

1. Donate to the food bank in your town every month, not just during the holidays.

2. List the birthdays of friends and family on a calendar on a day two weeks before the actual date. Your card will be sure to get there on time.

3. Write a letter to someone you haven't spoken to or heard from in a long time. Ask how they're doing. Give them cheerful news about yourself. Put little bright stickers all over the envelope. It might make their day.

4. Send a note to your kid's teacher saying how much you appreciate his or her time. Make it simple and ask for nothing. You'll keep the lines of communication wide open that way.

* * * * * *

5. Next time you go to a restaurant, if you enjoy the service and the food, leave more than just a tip. Make a list of reasons why your waiter did a good job and leave it alongside the tip. You will never be forgotten in that restaurant.

* * * * * *

Chapter Eleven
MY FAVORITE SEASON

There is no season when such pleasant and sunny spots may be lighted on, and produce so pleasant an effect on the feelings, as now in October.

—Nathaniel Hawthorne

Part of the joy of living is watching the seasons change. My favorite season is autumn. Maybe it comes from being a native of New England. When summer turns to fall in New England the change isn't subtle, it's spectacular. The air is crisp and seems cleaner. The leaves on the trees put on a show of color that even the squirrels have to stop and admire. When the afternoon sunlight of mid-October splashes through the deep reds and yellows of a Vermont forest, I'm convinced that if someone took a picture of heaven that's what it would look like.

I have two other names for this special season besides autumn: football season and fair season. Whether it's the local high school or a big time university, the sounds of pads popping against each other fill the autumn air on Friday nights and Saturday afternoons.

I've lived in the Northwest for the past 16 years, and my autumn routine begins in late August with a trip across the Cascade mountains to Washington State University. The rolling wheat fields of the Palouse are especially beautiful in the fall.

Another major highlight of this season is the Western Washington State Fair. It is also known as the Puyallup, since it takes place in a town by that name about 35 miles south of Seattle. I love everything about the fair. We arrive early for hot coffee and a scone, a traditional treat at the Puyallup. Then it's off to the animal barns to see the sheep, horses, cows, chickens and goats. They must think it strange that large groups of people come to visit them, but only once a year. "Where are those humans the rest of the time?" they must think.

When I lived in Connecticut I used to go to the Danbury Fair every fall. That's gone now. They put up a shopping mall where the fair stood for over 100 years.

My favorite part of the fair is the "Modern Living" building. As far as one can see there are sales people wearing little microphones pitching their products. I love to watch them work. That's fairly obvious, since I own three sets of kitchen knives that can cut through metal, two juicers, five jars of ring cleaner and two bottles of the stuff that keeps my glasses from steaming up.

When I lived in Connecticut I used to go to the Danbury Fair every fall. That's gone now. They put up a shopping mall where the fair stood for over 100 years. I hope that never happens in Puyallup.

One autumn tradition that has disappeared is the raking and burning of leaves. As a kid, we would rake them into large piles, jump in, then rake them up again and burn them. I love the smell of burning leaves, but outdoor burning isn't legal anymore. And rakes have been replaced by leaf blowers. They make too much noise and your arms don't even get much of a workout. And with all the pollution they pump out, the environment can sure take a beating.

More fall favorites. Fresh apple cider on Sunday afternoon. New fall clothes for school. Old fall clothes for school. The new car models, fall TV shows, the World Series and complaining about stores who put up Christmas decorations too early. I could go on forever, but I have to go blow the leaves into my neighbor's yard.

Focus Your Light

"For man autumn is a time of harvest, of gathering together" (Edwin Way Teale). See you at the fair!

* * * * * *

Chapter Twelve
PRIMING THE PUMP

Action will remove the doubt that theory cannot solve.

—Tehyi Hsieh

I could tell by the woman's eyes there was something wrong. She wasn't happy. She was attractive, usually smiling, and always had a nice greeting for her fellow workers, but now something was missing.

I had only met this woman a month earlier, but the words spilled out of my mouth anyway, "You're not really happy here, are you."

She was stunned, "How do you know that?" she said.

"I had that look once," I told her, "so I did something about it."

She wanted to hear the story, so we set up a meeting in the coffee shop later that day.

"I was cutting a customer's hair in my barber shop in my home town of Wilton, Connecticut, in 1971," I began. "I had a good business, nice customers, made a good living and my family was proud of me. But something was missing."

I explained how I used to look out the window and stare at the blue and red lines on the electric barber pole spiral endlessly upward. I looked at my own life that way, spiraling upward to a level of happiness and success beyond even my dreams. But I didn't know how to get there. I was scared.

Fear is like a prison wall. It stands between us and happiness. The big difference is this wall is created in our own minds and it's so high we can't see over the top, so we have no idea what's on the other side. We imagine bad things on the other side, so we find a way to avoid climbing the wall to find out.

Fear is like a prison wall. It stands between us and happiness. The big difference is this wall is created in our own minds and it's so high we can't see over the top, so we have no idea what's on the other side.

Fear definitely held me back from my childhood dream of being a radio and television sportscaster. The dream of having my own show, of creating new and fun ways to report sports, the dream of entertaining lots of people at the same time. At this stage of my life the fear was stronger than the dream. Fear told me I already had a good job. It was safe, secure. After all, my dad worked as a barber for over 60 years. It was an honest living.

Fear spoke loudly. It told me if I tried broadcasting I might fail. "So few people make it in that field," my friends told me.

Then it all changed. In my weekly perusal of self-help books I came across a story of a couple on a long hike. On a hot summer day they had gotten lost and wandered onto an old abandoned farm. Thirsty after walking more than 20 miles, the man reached into his backpack for some water. His plastic water bottle hadn't been capped tightly enough and was empty. His female companion had a full bottle of water and they could split that, but it wouldn't be enough for the long hike back. Just then the woman saw something on the corner of an old barn nearby, an old-fashioned water pump. She laughed and pumped it a couple of times but nothing came out. With one eye right up to the open end of the spout she said, "You know I heard somewhere, you have to prime and then you'll get water."

The couple had a problem. Should they prime the pump with their only supply of water and take a chance of getting enough to keep them going all day, or should they save the little they already had? It was a severe test of their faith. *Webster's New World Dictionary* defines "faith" as "unquestionable trust that does not require proof or evidence." To prime the pump could give them an abundant supply of cool, fresh water or perhaps nothing. To hang on to their bottle of water would be safe, and offer instant satisfaction, but nothing beyond that.

* * * * * *

The couple decided to go for it. They poured the water from their bottle into the pump, gave the handle a few hardy pushes and within seconds clear, fresh, cold water gushed from the spout.

That little tale of success is what I needed to hear. I decided to close my barber shop and pursue the broadcasting business. I took a job at a local radio station for half my salary as a barber—not a very sound financial move on the surface—but I had taken the "leap of faith" and had to believe the rest would work out.

I called my landlord to tell him I was going to move out of my shop, and before I could get a word out he said, "Tony, we have a problem. We need your rental space to enlarge the size of the bank vault next door. You're going to have to move. As compensation we are going to refund all your rent money for the past three years."

I was stunned. A miracle had happened. That refunded rent money would help supplement my income until I could get on my feet. I explained to the landlord, a long-time friend, that I was going to take a broadcasting job anyway. He appreciated my honesty and gave me a check for $4,000, my full rent for three years. So my career in broadcasting began.

My friend listened to my story intently and smiled broadly when I told her my true-life "leap of faith" story.

Three months after our conversation my friend and I said good-bye. She left for California and the job she'd always dreamed about. She decided to prime the pump, and water came flowing out.

Bright Idea
Set Goals

A. J. C. Penney said, "Give me a stock clerk with a goal, and I'll give you a person who will make history. Give me a person without a goal and I'll give you a stock clerk." Only about 3 percent of Americans take the time and effort to set goals and work to achieve them.

* * * * * *

B. To reach a goal you must "do what you have to do, when you have to do it, whether you like it or not." Whether you're running a marathon, climbing a mountain or struggling in math class, you must remember, ". . . if you go as far as you can see and then get there, you'll be able to see a little bit farther and go on" (Gene C. McKinney).

C. Here is my goal setting plan:

1. Figure out what your goal is. Write it down.
2. Ask yourself why you want this goal.
3. Identify what you need to know to make the goal happen.
4. Set a deadline and get started.
5. Work toward your objectives every day.

* * * * * *

Chapter Thirteen

THE LITTLE RED TRUCK

Those who bring sunshine to the lives of others cannot keep it from themselves.

—James Barrie

I've been fortunate enough to be able to generate enough Christmas memories to fill a dozen toy chests in the attic. Christmas 1955 was special. That year I wanted a little plastic red truck I had seen at Green's 5 and 10 in Norwalk, Connecticut.

The truck took two size "D" batteries in the storage bed. A little switch below the passenger door put the truck into motion. Well ahead of its time, the little truck had a front safety bumper. As soon as the truck hit the wall, a piece of furniture or Aunt Nettie's shoe, it would stop. Very cool for 1954, and I wanted one.

At this time, my family lived in a house on Ohio Avenue. The house had three small bedrooms and one bath. Somehow we all managed to use the bathroom without fighting. Some houses today have bathrooms for each child. How can a kid be normal with that kind of cushy childhood?

My big sister, Mary Jane, had one bedroom all to herself, and my younger sister, Bunny, and I shared a room. Bunny and I went to bed early on Christmas Eve. The theory was simple: when your time asleep goes faster, Christmas morning arrives much earlier. There was only one problem though: we couldn't sleep. Finally, though, around 8:45 p.m. I drifted off. I was awakened briefly by someone giving me a kiss on the cheek. At age 10 I was too old to believe in Santa Claus, which is strange because now I'm in my 50's and I still believe in Santa Claus. Anyway, Bunny insisted it was Santa, so I stayed with that thought.

Around 4:00 a.m. Bunny had to get up and go to the bathroom. She was only gone a few minutes when she came bounding back into the room. She bounced on my bed with an excited smile.

"You got it! You got the red truck!"

Well, so much for my Christmas surprise. If she had been a brother I would have slugged her for giving it away, but Bunny was so excited I had to forgive her. Besides, I was curious to know what else was under the tree.

We lay there on our beds for what seemed like a day and a half waiting for my father's Christmas signal. Every year he'd stand at the bottom of the stairs and give a simple whistle. That was our signal to bound toward the living room and slide toward the base of the tree. Another whistle allowed us to begin tearing at our gifts.

I never thought much about the whistle signal until I saw my dad call one of his dogs to go hunting. A simple whistle and the dog would bound into the car, proving that kids and dogs respond to love and to their owner's whistle. Dad was a whistler. It's a lost art today. Nobody whistles while they work anymore. Maybe whistling at a computer causes some virus because I never hear people whistle anymore.

Anyway, that Christmas was special to me and I'll never forget the little red truck. The image of my sister Bunny so excited to give me the news will stay with me the rest of my life. Christmas 1955 was the last Christmas we would spend together. My sister had been born with cystic fibrosis and died on March 12, 1956.

Now every Christmas Eve after everyone else has gone to bed, I kneel at the foot of the tree and pray out loud. "Hi Bunny. I miss you. I hope I get a little red truck this year." And I know she's smiling.

"Hey Mair, Elvis is on the phone."

I've always been a big fan of Christmas music. Every year I search for a Christmas CD or tape I don't have. The search is getting more and more difficult as my collection grows.

Neil Diamond, Perry Como, Johnnie Mathis, Kenny G, Reba McIntyre, Jim Nabors, Nat King Cole. The list goes on and on, but it would never be complete without my very first Christmas album

* * * * * *

by Elvis. There he is on the cover with that blue velour shirt and the Brylcream hairdo. I still have the original 33 rpm record album but have since bought a new CD version.

In my junior year in high school my sister, Mary Jane, went off to the University of Connecticut. On her first night back home for the holidays I was playing the Elvis Christmas album in my room. When "Santa Claus Is Back in Town" came on I turned up the volume. My sister came running from her room to tell me to shut it off.

"That is not Christmas music. That's awful. Turn that off."

The following year I had the same song playing when she arrived home for Christmas and the year after that too.

In 1965 Mary Jane got married and moved away. Three days before Christmas I called her at her new apartment and without saying a word played Elvis' "Santa Claus Is Back in Town." When the song ended I said, "Merry Christmas" and hung up.

Now more than 35 years later Elvis still sings to my sister. For the past 20 years the phone call has happened on Christmas Eve. No words are spoken. It's just Elvis singing "Santa Claus Is Back in Town." This past year my sister admitted, "I can't enjoy Christmas until I hear from Elvis."

For me it has never been about the gifts, except for that little red truck. Christmas for me will always be the image of my little sister Bunny smiling, my big sister Mary Jane waiting for the Elvis call, my dad's whistle, my brother Phil's annual grab bags for my kids and my sister's kids and my mother's quiet observation of all the happiness surrounding her on that holiday. She would always sum it up at the end of the Christmas dinner by saying out loud, "Thank you, God." That's what Christmas means to me.

Focus Your Light

Never take one single moment of this life for granted. Hug your sister today and if you don't have a sister, hug someone else's sister.

* * * * * *

Chapter Fourteen

DONUTS THE SIZE OF SOFTBALLS

You kids can have whatever you want.

—Grandpa Romano

I used to love to go to my grandpa's house. We would all pile into Dad's 1948 De Soto and drive north on Route 7 all day long. We were going to Vermont, a trip that even today takes about four hours from southern Connecticut. Improving roads in New England is something that town councils fight against as if it were the plague. Route 7 was, and still is, a winding snake of a highway, creeping slowly past such landmarks as Kent Falls, Connecticut, and Pittsfield, Massachusetts.

Once you get to Williamstown, Massachusetts, you're almost there. You can't miss that town. It's New England at its best—beautiful white clapboard buildings with black shutters. The campus of Williams College looks like a town Dickens created. Students dart from class to class in ivy-covered buildings under New England trees ablaze with color. Unless it's winter time, in which case they run from class to class under leafless trees dormant in their winter sleep. Or if it's spring, students wander from class to class amidst the sights and smells of nature's unveiling.

Only a mile or so past the campus Route 7 reaches Pownell, Vermont. "We're here!" we used to say, even though we still had 50 miles to go before we reached Rutland.

We would arrive at my grandfather's bakery in the late afternoon. Grandpa and Grandma Romano lived in an apartment above the bakery. A long flight of stairs led to their apartment. Arriving in the kitchen first, our noses would be rewarded. The aroma of spaghetti sauce filled the kitchen. Grandma always had something on the stove—and a lot of it. But there would be bigger and better aromas to come.

Grandma would put me in a bedroom toward the back of the house. It was small, but it had a window. The window didn't look outside, but the room was okay due to the location directly above the bread oven in my grandpa's bakery. Oh my!

Ordinarily, a motion on the pump handle would fill a donut to capacity, but that didn't satisfy me. I filled that first donut to the size of a softball. Grandpa just laughed and said "You can eat whatever you want here and there's milk in the refrigerator."

At exactly 3 o'clock in the morning every day the baker would arrive for work. By 4:30 a.m. the aroma of fresh baking bread would waft into my bedroom. A half hour later a large rectangular wire-mesh screen filled with donuts would be lowered into a vat of hot cooking oil. More wonderful smells. I had to get up. I had to go down there and see all of this close up. My eyes were filled with sleep, but my nose was filled with the magical aroma of donuts and pastries and pies. This was wonderland, more exciting than Yankee Stadium, at least for the moment.

As I walked slowly through the large work area of the bakery, I felt my grandfather's large hand clamp down on my shoulder. For a fleeting moment fear filled my 10-year-old heart. Was he going to yell at me for being in the bakery without permission?

"Good morning!" he yelled in a voice too loud for that hour. "You wanna work in the bakery?" he asked.

After my enthusiastic "yes," Grandpa led me over to the jelly donut filling machine. In those days there was nothing automated about it. It was a big hand pump with a pointy nozzle that stuck out of the side. You filled the pump from the top with jelly filling, stuck each donut on the little spout and started pumping. Ordinarily, a motion on the pump handle would fill a donut to capacity, but that didn't satisfy me. I filled that first donut to the size of a softball.

* * * * * *

Grandpa just laughed and said "You can eat whatever you want here and there's milk in the refrigerator."

To this day I cannot walk past a bakery without buying something, but they never let me fill the donuts. They must have heard about me from Grandpa.

Focus Your Light

Only in America do we stress over everything we eat. Drop everything you're doing right now and go eat a donut.

* * * * *

Mika and me at the Puyallup Fair

Mika and me

My Kids Pete, Lisa, Tim

Me and Rose
New Years Day - 1999

New York City Marathon
1984

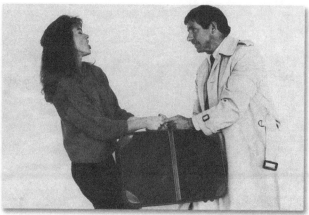

Dottie Dartland-now a writer for DHARMA AND GREG-
with me in a production of CHAPTER TWO

Rosehill Players' Danielle Hjotten

...me "shaking my bootie"
...with Camp Goodtimes kids

With Jennifer at Cystic Fibrosis event in 1992

With Jennifer at weight lifting benefit for Cystic Fibrosis

Mom at new place in Florida - Summer 2001

Brother Phil and wife Fran, Florida 1999

fly fisherman-my brother-in-law Earl

Danielle from Sammamish's Skyline High School arriving in Israel

Danielle and fellow Skyline classmates in Israel

First radio job
Westport, CT- 1971

KOMO Radio interview with University of Washington
Husky coach Don James- 1981

With Rosalynn Sumners
Helsinki, Finland - 1983

Me, Aaron Brown, Jean Enerson, Jeff Renner
KING 5 - 1983

KIRO TV - 1995
Harry Wappler, Steve Raible, Margaret Larson, me,
and crew

KIRO - Behind the scenes

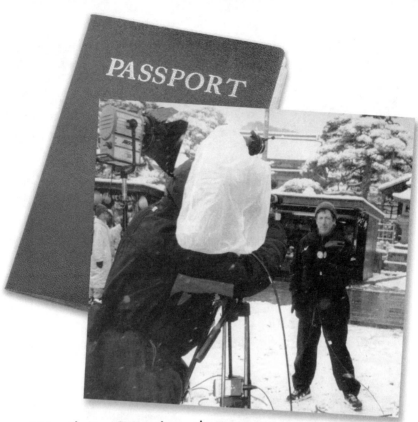

1998 Winter Olympics, Nagano, Japan

Seahawk Post Game Show
with longtime partner Sam Adkins

Kiro TV September 2001
Andy Wappler, Steve Raible, Susan Hutchison, me

Doing "Pep Talk" at an area business meeting

Me and the KCPQ Morning News crew,
Christine Chen and Walter Kelly

Dad and me
Seattle Waterfront
1993

Chapter Fifteen
FATHER'S DAY

The more you "pass on" to others, the more you keep for yourself.

—Unknown

I was lucky to be born into the home of Tony and Mary Ventrella on June 18, 1944. It happened to be Father's Day. Maybe that's why I was lucky to have such a good father.

My dad was a barber. From the first day of his working life to his last day on earth, he was a barber and proud of it. His parents migrated here from Italy in the early 1900s. My grandfather, Phillip Ventrella, worked in a hat factory in Norwalk, Connecticut. Every man wore a hat in those days. There were plenty of jobs.

Grandpa was pretty tough on his kids and my dad was independent, so he left home at the age of 16. Dad was a year shy of legal age but found a man to sign his dad's name so he could join the navy.

Of course, it didn't take long for the navy to discover Dad's true age. They encouraged him to go home with an honorable discharge, and that's when dad opened his first barber shop in Norwalk. He never had a boss. He worked for himself and was in charge of his own destiny for nearly 60 years. Even in his 80s he worked, but for another barber.

Dad would work on Saturdays to earn a little spending money. A very friendly guy, he always got a lot of tips and each Saturday evening when he came home, he put the tips on the kitchen table for my mom. He'd smile and say, "Here, Mary, this is for you." He was proud to still be able to "bring home the bacon."

My earlier memories of my dad go back to our first house on Truman Street in Norwalk. I'm sure he bought that house because the street was named after his second favorite president, Harry S. Truman. If there'd been a house on Roosevelt Street we would have bought that instead, I'm sure.

I remember waking up one night at the age of four to what I thought was a lion's roar. It turned out it was my dad snoring. What a relief. I don't think I could've handled a lion at the tender age of four.

Years later when Dad and I took his small camper to Vermont to go fishing, the lion returned. He slept in the bed by the door on one end of the camper, and I slept on the other end. In the middle of the night he began snoring and memories of the lion on Truman Street came back to life. I wasn't scared this time though. Instead, I was grateful to be spending time with my dad, even if he was sleeping.

My dad was not a big man, about 5'7", 170 pounds, but he loved hard work and worked like a big man. When I think of him now I see him digging a trench in the yard or cutting down a tree or weeding the garden he loved.

Dad was a hunter. He hunted rabbits in Vermont. He always hunted with dogs. Not just any dogs, Beagles. And not just any beagle, but Peggy. Peggy was my dad's favorite dog. She lived 13 years and brought him more pleasure than a million dollars could had provided.

"You were right to pursue your dream and leave the barber business." he said. "I have to admit I wasn't sure you could make it, but you did and I'm proud to say you were right."

One winter Dad lost Peggy in Vermont in a snow storm. I remember when he came home without Peggy. Dad couldn't sleep for a week. Every day he called the police station in the small town near the wooded area where Peggy got lost in a white out.

Dad phoned the many one-room school houses still in operation in Vermont in those days. Nothing. No word for a week, then two weeks. The weather in that part of Vermont that winter was bitter cold every night.

* * * * * *

Friends told my dad to forget about ever finding Peggy alive, but he wouldn't listen. Every weekend Dad went back to the spot where he'd lost sight of Peggy's tracks, calling her name for four hours until darkness set in. Two Sunday nights in a row he came back broken hearted. No sign of Peggy. Now he just wanted to find her so he could bury his old friend.

Then suddenly on Thursday of the third week, nearly 20 days after Peggy lost her way in that Vermont snow storm, Dad was given the first sign of hope.

"I think we've seen your dog," said a man with a thick New England accent over the phone, "but she won't let us near her."

"She'll never bite. Grab her." Dad told him, "It's probably Peggy."

A few minutes later the phone rang and my dad's face lit up. "They found her," he said, "She's alive, weak and her ribs are showing. She has even been eating out of the garbage, but she's alive."

The next day Dad drove back to Vermont to get Peggy. Her sad eyes seemed to sparkle for a brief second when she saw Dad reach down to pick her up.

Peggy lived three more years, even though it was estimated that she had survived temperatures of 20 below zero in the Vermont woods that winter.

Dad had other dogs in later years, some pretty good hunters, but none as close to his heart as Peggy.

———

When I left the barber business to enter the broadcasting field full time my dad wished me well, but as I left for the Midwest and my first job in television he stood in the driveway and said, "Keep your barber's license; don't ever let it run out." Deep down inside Dad thought the television broadcasting field was a bit suspect, not nearly as secure as barbering.

One day when I was visiting Dad and Mom in their house in Danbury, Connecticut, we were sitting at the table for breakfast and a strange thing happened. Dad reached across the table to shake my hand. He looked me straight in the eye and said, "You were right."

* * * * * *

I was baffled. All those years growing up as his son I was perfectly comfortable being wrong when he was right. I didn't know what he was talking about.

"You were right to pursue your dream and leave the barber business," he said. "I have to admit I wasn't sure you could make it, but you did and I'm proud to say you were right."

Well, I'm proud to say he was right. Right for teaching me to keep my feet on the ground. Right for showing me a lot more than how to do a haircut. Right for showing me how to treat people equally, no matter what race, color, income, social status or—God forbid—political party.

In July 1998, Dad and I made a fishing trip to Vermont. It would be our last trip together. He passed away three months later.

I wasn't much of a fly fisherman and dad knew it. He got a kick out of fishing a spot I just left and pulling a trout out of the water. But he wanted so badly to have me catch a fish and I never did.

That last night in the camper as I lay awake listening to his labored snoring I prayed to God for more time with my Dad, yet something told me that time was short.

Then on a beautiful October morning God came to get Dad. He must have known how much my dad loved the autumn. He must have known that every October Dad would say to us kids, "Well, the frost is on the pumpkin this morning." In all my years I've never actually seen a pumpkin with frost on it, but maybe I will someday.

Every Father's Day I hope two things. That my dad knew how much we loved him and always will. And that all young dads today will realize how unconditional love toward their children can shape the future of this world for generations to come.

* * * * *

Bright Idea
Never Give Up

A. A toddler wobbles across the floor and falls down. Seconds later he tries again and falls again. Does the toddler stop trying? If that baby is blessed with normal health he will try until he walks . . . a great lesson for adults who give up too easily.

B. When Sylvester Stallone wrote the script for the movie "Rocky," dozens of potential producers told him to go away. However, just like "Rocky," Stallone kept punching and refused to quit. Now he is one of the more successful actor-writers of all time.

C. In 1962, four nervous young musicians played their first record audition for the executives at Decca Record company. The executives were not impressed. While turning down the group, one said, "We don't like their sound. Groups of guitars are on their way out." The four young musicians refused to give up and millions of Beatles fans are still happy about that decision.

D. Bill Gates dropped out of Harvard, but he had a dream, a clear focus. He is now one of the wealthiest men in the world. More importantly, his computer genius has changed the world for the better.

E. Wilma Rudolph was the 20th of 22 children. Born prematurely, her survival was doubtful. When she was four years old she contracted double pneumonia and scarlet fever, which left her with a paralyzed leg. She had to walk with a brace. At age nine Wilma removed the brace and by 13 years old had developed a rhythmic walk. She decided to try running and in her first race finished last. Everyone told her to quit, but she kept on running. One day she won a race. Then she won another one. Eventually this little girl who was told she would never walk again went on to win three Olympic gold medals. Never give up!

* * * * * *

Chapter Sixteen
ROSE

Death is the supreme festival on the road to freedom.

—Dietrich Bonhoeffer

For years I'd been putting off my cookie baking lessons. Now in December of 1998 I would finally get my chance.

The occasion was bittersweet. My mother was spending her first Christmas without my dad since before they met nearly 70 years earlier. He had passed away in October, so I invited Mom to spend the holiday with us in Seattle.

As we pulled into Rose's driveway I was sure she and my mom would get along great. I was right. Rose met Mom with a hug at the front door just as she greeted all her guests.

The two women shared stories and laughs as they made Christmas cookies from scratch. I was familiar with Rose's cookies. I'd tasted them at New Year's Day parties at her house for the last three years. I felt as comfortable at her house as I did at my own mother's house growing up in Connecticut many years ago.

On New Year's Day, 1997, I asked Rose to give me cookie baking lessons. Months flew by and the lessons never happened. Finally in 1998, after having lost my dad, I made a promise to myself to get those cookie lessons from Rose.

Rose Obata was born in Seattle in 1929. She had lived in a cozy house on Capital Hill since 1960. Three children grew up under that friendly roof. Rose had lost her husband four years earlier and lived in the house with her daughter Chris since then.

I loved knocking on the door at Rose's house. You always knew that special treatment was waiting on the other side. The slightly built woman with short gray hair always had a big smile and a happy greeting for me and my wife Mika. She loved to talk about sports. Not superficial stuff either; she really knew her sports.

But we can't control time, we can't dictate how long our happy moments will last. We can only make the best of them while they last.

I always sat in my favorite leather chair near the fireplace and feasted on traditional holiday treats and a few of Rose's Asian delights too. Many times alone in that chair I wanted to freeze that moment—noisy happy sounds coming from the other room, great smells coming from the kitchen. I would've bottled it if I could have. I had the same feeling as Rose and Mom and I made Christmas cookies in December of 1998.

But we can't control time, we can't dictate how long our happy moments will last. We can only make the best of them while they last. Six months after our Christmas cookie session in Rose's kitchen, she was gone. She passed away of cancer in June of 1999. It took me three months to get up the nerve to tell my mom.

In her final weeks Rose taught us all about life. When it became obvious that all medical attempts to keep her alive had failed, she accepted her fate with a certain grace that became a life lesson for everyone she knew.

I remember driving to her house on what I expected would be my last visit. Rose was lying in bed greeting countless friends and relatives. As her son Greg later told me, "They'd arrive in tears and leave laughing." That's the way Rose made people feel even as she faced her own death.

* * * * * *

I tried to prepare something to say as I walked up the steps to her room. I came up blank. Then as I entered the room and saw Rose's smile I realized she'd done it again. She made me feel comfortable about something everyone fears. She looked up at me and said, "Isn't this crazy? I'd like to get this over with." She had decided that death is just a journey everyone has to take and she just wanted to get on with it.

I left the room with a smile on my face. Feeling at peace with her level of comfort and even feeling a little less fearful about my own mortality.

My Christmas cookies will never be as good as Rose's, but every December when I smell them baking in my oven I'll see Rose's face and feel that hug and be comforted by her presence in my heart and in my mind.

Focus Your Light

This holiday season ask an older relative or friend to help you learn something they already know. Two things will happen: you'll learn something new and they'll feel great about teaching you.

* * * * * *

Chapter Seventeen

THE HEALTH PLAN

The greatest thing in this world is not so much where we are, but in what direction we are moving.

—O. W. Holmes

There has been a lot of talk on both sides of the political aisle regarding health plans. What do Americans want? What do they need? How can we provide a reasonable health plan for everyone without making the lives of those in the medical profession miserable? No one seems to have the answer. So until someone does, I have a plan. It is called preventive maintenance.

An old mechanic friend of mine who smokes a pack and a half of cigarettes a day refuses to use anything but Pennzoil in his car. Does he care more about his car than he does about his body? It seems that way. Come to think of it, a body can be compared closely to a car. A body has filters like a car. Instead of an oil filter, you have kidneys. What about the liver, the heart, the lungs? They too have counterparts in the automobile that also need to be taken care of. Nobody is disease proof, but it makes sense to do all you can to stay healthy. Just don't drink Pennzoil.

Statistics prove we're going to be dead a lot longer than we're alive, so let's enjoy as healthy a life as possible.

In 1984, I ran the New York City Marathon. The 26.2-mile race weaves through all five boroughs of New York City, a wonderful experience for the runner. The race is run in late October or early November and traces of New England's brilliant colors are still on display in Central Park as one completes the long journey.

The day before the race I was standing in the lobby of the Sheraton Hotel interviewing runners from all over the world. Working as Sports Director for KING-TV in Seattle, I was able to be a running reporter for this event.

I listened, as runners from England, Germany, Ireland and Japan told me why they had come to New York for this race. An elderly man stepped forward and interrupted. "I'd like to tell my story," he said.

"I'd like to listen." I replied, and for the next half hour 84-year-old Noel Johnson filled my ear with a fascinating story of one man's crusade to change his life.

"They canceled my life insurance when I was 70," he told me. "I had everything wrong with me, bad heart, bad lungs. I couldn't sleep, and I felt lousy all the time."

Noel was about five feet, seven inches tall with a dark tan and thick white hair. His grip was firm, his blue eyes clear, his smile bright. He didn't have an ounce of fat on him, and I was sure he had been an athlete all his life, but I was wrong.

"They canceled my life insurance when I was 70," he told me. "I had everything wrong with me, bad heart, bad lungs. I couldn't sleep, and I felt lousy all the time."

After a stern warning from his doctor, Noel decided to make some changes. He quit smoking, cut down on drinking, put aside some of the high-fat foods he was eating and, most important, he began to exercise.

"First I walked half a block. That's all I could make. Then a quarter of a mile, a half mile, a full mile, but soon I became bored."

That's when Noel began jogging. Within a year he was jogging in short races. He was 71 then and it was easy to finish in the top ten of his age group. Only two years after he started jogging, Noel ran his first marathon. When I met him in 1984, the New York City marathon was his twentieth race.

Race day was a gem. Bright sunny skies greeted us as we boarded buses from the hotel out to the Verazano Narrows Bridge where Mayor Koch and Race Director Fred Lebow, would fire the cannon

* * * * * *

signaling the start of the race. There were more than 20,000 runners that day; I knew I would not find Noel Johnson until the finish.

"Boom!" The sound of the cannon startled me and the race was under way. The bridge was so packed with runners that we actually walked the first half mile, but by the time we stepped into Brooklyn we were jogging and it was already hot.

The clear October skies allowed the early autumn sun to drive the temperature a little higher than more marathoners wanted that day. By the time we hit Wall Street at the 20-mile mark, it was almost 80 degrees.

More than 200 runners dropped out of the race that day, but thanks to months of training and some encouragement from people along the streets, I made it to the finish line 3 hours and 47 minutes after I started. Where was Noel, I thought. Did he make it? Did he beat me? I had to find him.

I wandered through the recovery area in Central Park for almost an hour and saw people sitting under trees quietly celebrating their survival in the heat. Some ate fruit, others poured water over their heads and gazed straight ahead, perhaps enjoying that "runner's high" we all talk about. But no sign of Noel.

Later that night I showered and ate a quiet dinner in my room at the Sheraton. Still hungry for dessert, I walked across the street to the famous Lindy's Deli for a piece of their incredible cheesecake. I figured I could forget about the fat, having just run 26 miles.

As I enjoyed a wedge of my favorite dessert, I glanced into a corner and saw Noel Johnson. All alone at a table, he seemed dejected. I walked over and took a chair next to my 84-year-old running pal as he looked up at me with a frown.

"How'd you do today Noel?" I asked him.

"I'm not happy." said Noel. "For the first time in my running career I had to quit before the finish. I dropped out at 18 miles, I'm so disappointed."

I looked at him and smiled. "Noel, you've run 20 marathons. You're 84 years old, and it was 80 degrees today. What's the problem? Give yourself a break."

* * * * * *

Noel thought for a moment, then replied, "You're right, and besides, if I didn't have to run the San Diego Marathon next Sunday I would've finished today. I just wanted to save my strength."

Noel invited me to breakfast in the hotel lobby the next morning. He had a gift for me. As we sat at the table, laughing and joking about the hottest NYC marathon in history, he handed me a book he had written earlier that year. As I looked at the title I had to laugh: "A Dud at 70, a Stud at 80, the Story of Noel Johnson."

Now anytime I'm out running and begin to feel tired, I think of that 84-year-old man who took control of his life and changed it forever. No degree of bickering in Congress will prevent people like Noel—or any of us—from creating our own health plan by taking care of ourselves.

Bright Idea
Maintain Good Health

A. When my grandma was 90 years old, she started running five miles a day. Now we don't know where she is. Only kidding. The point is, it is never too late to start an exercise program. The key to success is to challenge yourself and no one else. Start slowly. Walk a short distance the first day, maybe half a mile. Do that for two weeks before you increase the distance by a quarter mile each time. If that gets boring walk faster and time yourself. Still bored? Start jogging. Let me know if you see my grandma.

B. Watch your diet. Actually I don't like the word "diet." The first three letters are "DIE." So forget that word for a minute. Instead, let us call it a healthy eating plan. Load up on fresh fruits and vegetables. Drink as much water as you can get into your system without actually springing a leak. Make a list of what you eat for one full week. Ask your doctor to evaluate the list and let him or her help you figure out what might be added or subtracted to help you attain a more healthy eating plan.

* * * * * *

C. Picture this: you own a beautiful race horse, a chestnut colt. He's running around your big back yard right now. How proud you are. Boy, he has to be worth a million bucks at least. Think about this: would you let him stay up all night smoking cigarettes and drinking booze? I don't think so. Well, what about your own body, that must be worth way more than a million dollars. If you don't believe me, consider this question: Would you trade your eyes for a million dollars? How about five million? Ten or more? Of course not. Would you give me one of your legs for five million? I don't think so. See, you're already worth at least 15 million and we haven't even gotten to the arms.

Chapter Eighteen
WIFFLE® BALLS
FROM THE PAST

People rarely succeed at anything unless they have fun doing it.

—Anonymous

I got a letter the other day. It made me laugh and cry at the same time. The letter came from a friend I haven't seen in 21 years. There was a group of four that used to hang out at my old barber shop in Wilton, Connecticut. I ran the shop; the other three guys were frequent customers.

The letter came from Mark, a clothing salesman in Rhode Island. Back then he was the red-headed kid who actually could hit my Wiffle® curve ball occasionally.

Another member of the group was Eddie. A curly haired blonde with a great sense of humor. He liked to argue just for the sake of it. That may explain why he's an attorney in Maine now.

Rounding out the group that summer of 1971 was Paul Crane. As a teenager he came to my shop for haircuts. I was beginning a career in radio then and Paul used to love to come to WMMM to see what the business was all about. Apparently, he liked what he saw. He's on CNN sports now.

The four of us did everything together that summer. There were those two-on-two Wiffle® Ball games out behind the barber shop. Customers had to wait until the end of the inning to get their haircut.

There was the day Paul broke his nose going after a fly ball. He ran right into a big tree in left field. We washed his face off in the shampoo sink. By the way, he made the catch.

A letter is a spirit builder, a mood changer. It's like opening your mailbox and finding an old friend.

There was the trip to Vermont and a night at the Green Mountain race track. We put five bucks each on one number and the horse threw his jockey coming out of the starting gate. We laughed until we cried. Neither horse or jockey was hurt. We lost our money though.

All the memories came back when I read Mark's letter. What a treat it was. We're planning a reunion at the Rutland Fair. I'm sure a Wiffle® Ball game is in the works too.

In this day of fax machines, personal computers, and cellular phones, it's nice to get a letter occasionally, not one of those computer updates people send out with their Christmas cards, but a real letter.

A letter is a spirit builder, a mood changer. It's like opening your mailbox and finding an old friend.

I wrote back to Mark a few days later. I thanked him for all the memories and suggested we meet soon for old times' sake. I can't wait to hear from him again. I hope he doesn't send me a fax or an email.

Focus Your Light

Just once in the coming year plan to do something crazy. Play three rounds of golf in the same day, leave work in the middle of the day and take some co-workers to the zoo or order a big cake when it's nobody's birthday and nobody is leaving the company.

* * * * *

Chapter Nineteen
JENNIFER, THE SMALLEST ANGEL

One person with courage makes a majority.

—Andrew Jackson

On August 7, 1999, another angel got her wings. That's the day my friend Jennifer passed away. She was only 13. She reminded me so much of my sister Bunny who also died at a young age.

I met Jennifer in the fall of 1991. We were doing a promotional spot for the Cystic Fibrosis Foundation Stair Climb. This energetic six-year-old came bouncing up to me outside the Washington Mutual Tower and said, "Hi, I'm Jennifer. Are you going to put me on TV?" We were buddies from that moment on.

In that first promo Jennifer was stationed at the top of the 57 flights of steps in the Washington Mutual Tower. A camera followed me up every flight until I reached the top completely out of breath. Jennifer stood there with her stop watch, looked at me, looked at the camera and in a seasoned actor's voice said, "Too slow, Tony. Do it again." We did the promo in one take. She was that good.

In the years that followed I got to know her dad, Eric, and her mom, Terry. I knew the struggle they were going through every day of their daughter's life because I had watched my own parents face that same awful reality years before. You simply never knew how long your child was going to live.

As I got to know Jennifer through other Cystic Fibrosis events, it was clear that her presence made me feel alive and more appreciative of every day of my own life.

For a year or so before she died, Jennifer's family had her on a donor list for a new set of lungs. A procedure only recently successful, the lung transplant had already saved the lives of many cystic fibrosis patients. Jennifer and her parents made several trips to Stanford University in California to prepare for such a transplant.

As time passed and no donors became available, Jennifer's condition worsened. She made frequent trips to Children's Hospital in Seattle to have her lungs drained and I visited her on many of those occasions. I always found her in good spirits, even though I sensed that her condition was worsening.

A 13-year-old explained in a simple one-page letter why she chose to yield to God's will rather than "prolong the pain and suffering" of her parents and friends. "God meant me to have these lungs," she explained, "and I accept that. I am not afraid. I am going to be with God."

Jennifer's mom and dad never complained and were always so appreciative of everyone in their large and loving circle of family and friends. In June of 1999 they invited my wife, Mika, and I to Jennifer's 13th birthday party. As we stood and talked with Eric, he informed us that Jennifer had chosen not to have the lung transplant. He masked his broken heart by stating matter-of-factly that Jennifer didn't want any more shots or any more hospital visits.

As we left the house that day, I knew that meant this child had made a deal with God to come home and leave her earthly suffering behind. A week or two later I took Jennifer and her best friends to a Mariners game at the brand new Safeco Field. They met some players and had a ball. Then we spent a day at GameWorks, a downtown Seattle amusement center.

The following week I called Jennifer's mom to ask if I could spend some time with Jennifer and try to talk her into having the lung transplant. She agreed.

* * * * * *

When I got to the house Jennifer was eager to show me some new Beanie Babies she had gotten and we shared some french fries and a Coke. Then I asked her why she had decided not to have the surgery. Jennifer looked at me for a moment, smiled and said, "Let me explain it to you at another time, Tony." I didn't press the issue further.

Jennifer died less than a month after my visit. At her funeral her Mom handed me a letter. She said quietly, "Jennifer wanted to explain her decision in a letter instead of in person."

I couldn't look at the letter until a few days later. I won't share the exact contents now, but I will say this. A 13-year-old explained in a simple one-page letter why she chose to yield to God's will rather than "prolong the pain and suffering" of her parents and friends. "God meant me to have these lungs," she explained, "and I accept that. I am not afraid. I am going to be with God."

Tears filled my eyes when I read the letter but they were soon replaced by a sense of gratitude for knowing this special person, Jennifer. She taught me to live every day as the special gift it is. She taught me to smile more, to laugh and to grab hold of the joy that some people mistake for "everyday life."

A month or so after Jennifer's death her parents sent me a photo and a poem. Here's the poem:

I'm Free

Don't grieve for me, for now I'm free
I'm following the path God laid for me.
I took his hand when I heard him call
I turned my back and left it all.
I could not stay another day
to laugh, to love to work and play.
Tasks undone must stay that way
I found that peace at close of day.
If my parting has left a void
Then fill it with remembered joy.

* * * * *

A friendship shared, a laugh, a kiss,
ah yes, these things I too will miss.
Be not burdened with times of sorrow.
I wish you the sunshine of tomorrow.
My life's been full, I've savored much,
good friends, good times, a loved one's touch.
Perhaps my time seemed all too brief.
Don't lengthen it now with undue grief.
Lift up your hearts and share with me
God wanted me now: He set me free.

Focus Your Light

It says in the Bible, "and a little child shall lead them" (Isaiah 11:6). Take the time to listen to the wisdom of a child. Don't talk, just listen.

* * * * * *

Chapter Twenty

"YOU'VE GOT A FACE FOR RADIO"

The man who wins may have been counted out several times, but he didn't hear the referee.

—H. E Jansen

Tampa, Florida, is about to become very small as my plane jets to 10,000 feet and eventually 35,000 feet en route to Pittsburgh, PA. When I fly US Airways I always go through Pittsburgh. I love the airport—lot's of stores and places to eat. Looks like a mall, except everyone has luggage. I'll be in Pittsburgh for an hour before taking off for Seattle. That should give me enough time to pick up another Pittsburgh Steelers shot glass for my wife. She doesn't drink much and couldn't care less about the Steelers, but she'll get a laugh out of the glass.

Just 24 hours ago I walked with my mom down to the dock at Balmoral Assisted Living Facility in Palm Harbor, Florida. Mom is 88 years old and still pretty spry. Just a month ago she left Connecticut to come to Florida. Now she's closer to my older brother, Phil, and his wife Fran. She loves Fran. Everyone does. It was Fran who found this new home for mom. It was Fran who spent a week with curtains, bedspreads and little knickknacks making the new place look like home. Now they use my mom's apartment as a model for prospective new residents.

As we walked back into the dining area, we passed a man moving slowly to the elevator with a walker. Just a week ago I visited a friend with a toddler, and suddenly the 90-year-old man and the toddler had something in common. They both relied on that walker to get around.

It made me think. The toddler needs the walker to help him with his first steps. The old man needs the walker to help with his final steps. It's reality. In between the one-year-old child and the 90-year-old man is a lifetime. During that lifetime we have so many decisions to make. Decisions that if made differently would have changed the course of our lives. The wonderful mystery is we never really know where our decisions will take us until we make them.

———

In 1972, after working in the haircutting business for eight years I made the decision to pursue a career in radio sports broadcasting and sports writing for a local newspaper. I closed the door of my barber shop and went to work for WMMM radio in Westport, Connecticut, doing morning sportscasts every 15 minutes. I also landed a high-paying job at the *Wilton Bulletin*, a weekly newspaper in my home town.

Since it was a weekly, I worked only on Mondays writing and editing the entire sports section. My pay was $25 a week. Don't laugh—it was a car payment in 1972.

I worked at WMMM for four and a half years before moving to the town next door and competitor station WNLK. The most notable thing I did at WMMM was break into music programming to announce that Richard Nixon had resigned as President. Then to take the edge off the moment I threw in a couple of baseball scores.

———

At the end of my sixth year in radio I decided to give television a shot. My boss told me I'd never make it in television. He said I didn't have the look.

At the end of my sixth year in radio I decided to give television a shot. My boss told me I'd never make it in television. He said I didn't have the look. He was half right. I still don't have the look, but I've just completed my 25th year in television.

I had a friend who worked for a television consultant in Stamford, Connecticut. I put on the only suit I owned and went to his office

* * * * * *

to make a video resume tape. I kept it simple. It was just me sitting at a table describing how stressful it was to park a car at Yankee Stadium. Two minutes of stand-up comedy, except I was sitting down. I mailed a copy of the tape to three television stations, Salt Lake City, Sacramento and Fort Wayne. The first two didn't even respond. They apparently agreed with my old boss about my chances of making it in the television business.

On a Monday morning about a month after sending out the tapes I was sitting alone at my desk at WNLK Radio on the verge of giving up my broadcasting career. I must have looked pathetic sitting there because a voice broke the silence: "Hey Tony, you look like you're about to jump out a window." It was a friend who worked in the sales

> *I'll be honest with you. Your resume tape sucked— terrible production, bad lighting, poor color—but I like your personality. Can you fly out here?"*

department. Her short red hair and bright smile lifted me out of my self-imposed misery.

"I give up," I said, "I'm going back to haircutting. No television station is going to hire me." Her eyes opened wide and she said, "Oh, stop. Don't give up now. See what happens in another week or so. I think you'll get a job." She patted me on the head and left the room.

The next morning I was alone at my desk again when the phone rang. "Hi, this is Ian Pearson, News Director at WANE TV in Fort Wayne, Indiana. I'd like to talk to you about the job we've posted."

I was stunned. I couldn't speak. I didn't have to because he continued. "Tony, I'd like to fly you out here in a day or so and have you audition for me on the set. I'll be honest with you. Your resume tape sucked—terrible production, bad lighting, poor color—but I like your personality. Can you fly out here?"

Two days later I was in Fort Wayne, Indiana, sitting on a television set with two people I'd never seen before in my life. My audition was mediocre at best. I thought I'd blown my opportunity.

I got back home and waited. My red-headed sales friend kept encouraging me. Every day the same message, "Don't you ever give up, Tony."

* * * * * *

Then it happened. My phone rang. It was Ian Pearson again. "Tony, I'd like to offer you the job."

Without even asking about the pay, hours, vacation, benefits or number of snack machines, I accepted. Three weeks later I left my home in New England for the corn and soybean fields of northeast Indiana.

I had been on the job only a month when a friend from WNLK called to tell me that my dear red-headed sales friend had passed away from cancer. I was stunned. "How long did she know she was sick?" I managed to say. "About four months, Tony."

My God, what courage it took for her to stand there and tell me to be patient and keep the faith when all along she knew she was dying. I truly believe I have a team of angels looking after me. In my mind I see my angels as stars in the night sky. She's the one with the red tint and that special sparkle that must be her smile.

After five years in Fort Wayne, covering everything from Little League baseball to the best high school basketball I'd ever seen, I applied for a job in Seattle. In September 1981 with my hair still in an experimental perm my brother had given me, I appeared on the air at KOMO TV for the first time.

"In order to succeed you must know what you're doing, like what you're doing and believe in what you're doing."

Now, 20 years later, I've worked at KING TV and KIRO TV and have enjoyed every minute of my sports career. I've had the chance to cover the World Figure Skating Championship in Finland, the summer Olympic Games in Seoul, Korea, the winter Olympic Games in Nagano, Japan, and many other memorable events.

Throughout my broadcasting career I've had the privilege of speaking in front of hundreds of schools, companies, service groups and political events. I've been able to share stories about people who have inspired me, encouraged me, taught me and cared about me.

Through my connections in the broadcasting field I was able to form a theatre group 17 years ago and produce and take part in over 25 plays with my friend and partner, David Blacker.

* * * * * *

I've met people I never would have met, seen events I never would have seen and was touched by lives that otherwise would have been unknown to me.

Now, as I watch the 90-year-old man make his way slowly into the elevator with his walker, I wonder how many memories he carries with him and I pray they will comfort him.

I also wonder what might be next for me. Is there something else I should be doing? Have I done enough in this world? Have I done all I wanted to do? It's funny, the last time I had this many questions I was sitting alone at my desk at WNLK staring at the telephone.

I think it's time to contact my angels again. Outside the airplane window I see them all, all the stars I've picked out and named. One for my sister Bunny, who died when she was 10 and I was 11. One for my dad, who left us October 19, 1998, one for Jennifer, the courageous 13-year-old girl who became an angel in August 1999 and one for Rose, my spirited and loving friend who said goodbye at 70 that same summer. They're all out there and I'm sure one of them has the answer.

Bright Idea
Take Responsibility for Your Actions

Every week I get at least three phone calls from college or high school students asking about the sports broadcasting business. They want to know how I got started and how they can get started.

Often when I tell them how I got started they're not so sure they even want to get started.

Here's what I tell them. "In order to succeed you must know what you're doing, like what you're doing and believe in what you're doing." But there's more. As my high school principal told me on graduation night June 16, 1962, "You must be willing to do what you have to do when you have to do it whether you like it or not."

* * * * * *

Most people spend more time planning how to get a job than they spend learning and perfecting the job once they have it.

In broadcasting, as in most other occupations, it is important to learn something new every day. The day you think you know everything marks the beginning of the end of your career.

———

The rules for finding success in any business are the same:

1. Always give more effort than you are paid to give.

2. Never complain in front of fellow workers. Nobody cares and it'll get back to someone who is in a position to alter your employment status in a hurry.

3. When you're in a meeting listen to others' suggestions before you offer one of your own. Always give credit to those who speak before you then offer your own ideas.

4. Don't gossip. It's a waste of your time and a waste of the company's time and money.

5. Always try to learn something new every day about your chosen business.

6. When speaking about your company among outsiders always say positive things.

7. If you're a manager remember this: "When you hire people who are smarter than you are, you prove you are smarter than they are" (R. H. Grant).

Most important—whether you already have a job in your chosen profession or you're seeking one—remember one of my favorite quotes: "Shoot for the moon. Even if you miss you'll land among the stars" (Les Brown).

* * * * * *

Chapter Twenty-one

PAUSING FOR
THE FIRE SIGNAL

The thing about performance, even if it's only an illusion, is that it is a celebration of the fact that we do contain within ourselves infinite possibilities.

—Daniel Day Lewis

I was sitting at my desk at KING-TV in the spring of 1986 when the phone rang. "We love you and Aaron Brown on KING-5 and wondered if you guys would like to play Oscar and Felix in a community production of *The Odd Couple* this summer. That marked the beginning of the Rosehill Players, a wonderful community theater group in Mukilteo, Washington.

As it turned out, we didn't do *The Odd Couple* until 1987, but we did do a production of Herb Gardner's *A Thousand Clowns* and had a fantastic time putting that together.

After that show my close friend, David Blacker, and I formed a new theater group in the old Rosehill School on Lincoln Avenue. We've produced a play there every summer ever since.

Growing up in Wilton, Connecticut, I saw several productions at the Wilton Playshop on Lover's Lane. (Yes, it's really called Lover's Lane.) And ever since I stepped on the stage at the Bonner Playhouse near Redding in the summer of 1968, I've been in love with community theater.

So when I came to the Northwest to take a television job I knew I would eventually be involved in theater again. Little did I know it would happen on the site of Territorial Governor Isaac Stevens' signing of the Point Elliott Treaty of 1855.

Built in 1928, the Rosehill School was home to elementary and junior high school students until its doors closed in 1973. The building sat idle for three years until in 1976 it became the Rosehill Community Center.

The stage used for Rosehill Players productions is in the gym. Theater goers sit on hard folding chairs and endure terrible acoustics, occasional outdoor sounds, and often on bright summer evenings streaks of sunlight crossing their line of sight to the stage. But they keep coming back for more.

"I've seen every one of your shows," a woman told me at a grocery store recently. "I especially loved you in 'Morons.'" I thanked her with a smile, even though the show she referred to was actually called Fools.

"I've seen every one of your shows," a woman told me at a grocery store recently. "I especially loved you in 'Morons.'" I thanked her with a smile, even though the show she referred to was actually called *Fools*.

Through the years the Rosehill Players have welcomed some wonderful actors and crew members to the fold, people who have changed our lives and their own. One of my favorites is Irene Griffore, a British war bride who survived the Nazi Blitzkrieg in London as a child. As our property mistress in several shows, Irene would always tell us, "The difficult can be done immediately; the impossible will take a little longer."

Then there's Billie, a middle-class, middle-aged schoolbus driver whose confidence level was so low she had trouble facing her own children. After a starring role in *Fools*, Billie told David Blacker, "This changed my life. I'm so much more confident now. I love to make people laugh."

Little 10-year-old cutie Danielle Hjorten appeared one day to audition for a part in *Jake's Women* and wowed audiences that summer with her performance.

* * * * * *

Veteran film and television actor Marni King took a role in *George Washington Slept Here* and began a relationship with my long-time friend, David Dilgard. They're happily married now.

One day we got a call from 10-year-old Jake Ehrler. "I'd like to volunteer to work in your theater," Jake said. "I'll do anything." He was right. Jake did an excellent job with his role in *The Nerd* and later became a valuable asset backstage, even helping to direct a show.

As our property mistress in several shows, Irene would always tell us, "The difficult can be done immediately; the impossible will take a little longer."

Of the people who have crossed the Rosehill stage since 1986, though, Dottie Dartland is our most famous alumna. Dottie was the last woman to audition for a part in Neil Simon's *Chapter Two* in 1988. She was working as a waitress at the old Seahorse Restaurant on the Mukilteo waterfront. She got the part after one reading and mesmerized local audiences for the next five weekends.

I'll never forget the confused look in Dottie's eyes when David told us to be sure to pause for the fire signal. In those days the Mukilteo fire station was next door to the stage. In any fire emergency a very loud signal went off to call in the volunteers. One Friday night in the middle of a dramatic scene from *Chapter Two*, that signal pierced the night air and the ears of everyone in the audience. Dottie and I held character for what seemed like 20 minutes. Then when the signal stopped we continued. The audience gave us a polite moment of applause, perhaps to say, "That must have been tough . . . good job."

After the show Dottie moved to California to get her master's degree in playwriting from the University of California at Davis. With degree in hand she drove her 1980 Ford Torino to Los Angeles to seek a career in film writing. After selling a script to ABC for

* * * * * *

their award-winning series, *China Beach*, Dottie found success. In the mid-nineties Dottie and some other writers created a hit show called *Caroline in the City*, and they followed that with a blockbuster television series called *Dharma and Greg*. Dottie lives with her husband Eric in Malibu. She's working on a new comedy, and we won't be shocked if it's a hit too.

All the people who have strolled across the Rosehill stage or toiled backstage have a special place in their hearts for the old place. Unfortunately, at the end of 2003 the Rosehill curtain will close for the final time, giving way to the wrecking ball. It won't take long for the building to be reduced to broken boards and a plume of dust, but not even progress can chase away the cherished memories of the Rosehill stage.

Somewhere in our memories and everywhere in our hearts will be the thunderous laughter, the silent tears, the opening night jitters, the closing night blues, and all the emotions in between that made the Rosehill Community Center and the Rosehill Players a cherished part of our lives.

Focus Your Light

See if your town has a community theatre. If not, find one in a nearby town. Find out who's in charge and volunteer to work on the next production. Better yet, audition for a part in the next production. It could change your life. . . .

* * * * * *

Chapter Twenty-two
THE SENIOR CLASS

Age is strictly a case of mind over matter. If you don't mind, it doesn't matter.

—Jack Benny

In 1960 after the New York Yankees lost the World Series to the Pittsburgh Pirates in seven games, manager Casey Stengal was fired. At 70 years of age the management called him "too old." Quoted in the daily news the next day, Stengal simply said, "I'll never make the mistake of being 70 again."

That was Casey's clever way of letting all the young executives know that someday they too would be 70, if they were lucky.

By the year 2010 there will be more people 60 years old and older than ever before in the history of the United States. That's right, just a few years from now almost 50 million people will be 60 or more. What does that mean to you and me besides the fact that Denny's will be the most crowded restaurant in America?

It means plenty. It means we'd better have healthcare plans that are affordable to all seniors. It means we'd better have housing, transportation, education, marketing, advertising, television programming, and entertainment aimed at seniors. It makes good business sense and it is the right thing to do.

But, besides all that, older people are the windows to the future for the young. Seniors are a wonderful resource. So full of knowledge and experience. So fascinating to listen to. They've been where we're going. Their faces show it, their eyes show it, their conversation proves it.

Most of us have had little experience with older people. Oh sure, we all kissed Grandma and Grandpa on holidays. We took that dollar bill,

> *Older people are the windows to the future for the young. Seniors are a wonderful resource. So full of knowledge and experience.*

the pinch on the cheek, and the advice on saving money, but did we really listen beyond that? I know I didn't. I didn't listen or observe much until my own parents turned 80 a few years back. Suddenly, everything they had to say was clever or funny or insightful.

My mother lives in Florida at a wonderful senior apartment complex near Tampa. When I visit her I try to observe some of the other people. Last summer on a short visit I talked with a man wearing a Boston Red Sox baseball cap. He had pitched in the high minor leagues in the 1930s. He told me he repeatedly hit batters who stood too close to the plate. "I'd stick it right in their ear," he said with a glow in his aging eyes.

Sitting alone in a chair on her first day at the facility was a gracious lady named Virginia. She had a wonderful southern accent, and the soft smooth skin on her face suggested that years earlier she had been capable of stealing men's hearts. She talked of her home in the south, of missing her family, and of being a little uncomfortable in her new surroundings. But as she talked of her life in the south, a smile crossed her face. She was seeing pictures of her past as she described them to me.

On my way out of the building that first day I ran into a lively man in a wheelchair. He was smoking a pipe. In a deep and powerful voice he asked my name. When I told him I was Mary Ventrella's son he broke into a song, "Ooee Marie, Ooee Marie!" His voice was filled with joy, and he said with a smile, "Your mother is really something."

He spoke of his family in the Northeast and shrugged his shoulders when he said how much he missed them. Then, as I turned to leave, he said, "But life is good, Tony, life is good," and he began to sing again.

* * * * * *

When I was growing up in Connecticut my father had a good friend thirty years his senior. We knew the man as Mr. Abbott. In fact, we called him "Old Man Abbott." Until I was twelve I thought his first name was actually "Old Man."

Mr. Abbott let us snoop around his attic where we found *National Geographic* magazines from the early 1900s. He let us go into the garage outside his house and open the hood of his old Packard.

My mother invited Mr. Abbott to our house for every major holiday. He had no family, so we were his family. A Yale graduate in the early 1900s, Mr. Abbott was a wonderful source of knowledge, humor, and friendship for all of us. Looking back, I appreciate him so much more now.

Our citizens of age have a lot to offer. We must learn from them, share with them, talk to and listen to them, and cherish them, for some day soon we'll be among them.

Bright Idea
Get Involved

A. Call a senior services agency in your area and become a volunteer; there are so many ways you can help.

B. Make a point to visit an elderly neighbor once a week.

C. Offer to mow a lawn, clean up a garage, or just play cards.

D. Someday if we're lucky we'll all be seniors, and we'll welcome a friendly face and a helping hand.

* * * * * *

Chapter Twenty-three
SHAKE YOUR BOOTIE

Laughter is the shortest distance between two people.

—Victor Borge

They gather on a Sunday in late June at a small summer camp on Vashon Island in Washington. They spill out of cars and vans from all across the state. Some smile, some frown, a few even cry. But by the end of their incredible week the smiles and tears blend together to create a pool of emotions that stay with them for a lifetime.

Welcome to Camp Goodtimes. Founded by Charlotte Ellis in 1983, the camp is for young cancer patients ages seven to seventeen and accepts 125 campers every summer. "It is our goal to give every child with cancer a week at camp," Charlotte said the first time I met her.

There is so much joy attached to a week at Camp Goodtimes that over 20 percent of the staff are former campers themselves. They can't stay away. They must come back and serve.

I was first introduced to Camp Goodtimes by a young lady named Annie in 1986. She had been a camper and was now a staff member. As I left the ferry dock and drove to the small camp nestled in the trees above Puget Sound, I tried to imagine what I would see there. Would the kids have no hair? Would they be in wheelchairs? Or worse yet would they be going through the motions of having fun to make their parents feel better? I really didn't know. But it all became clear to me when I sat down for lunch in the cafeteria.

Suddenly everyone in the room was pointing to me and yelling for me to stand up and dance. After a short demonstration by some of the boys at my table I got up and tried to dance to chants of "Shake Your Bootie."

My bootie has little chance of making it to the dance hall of fame, and soon everyone in the room was laughing. Suddenly I felt at ease at Camp Goodtimes. "Wow," I said out loud to myself, "all these kids are having a ball."

I spent the rest of the day as one of the kids. I had my face painted, played basketball, raided one of the cabins, tossed a few water balloons, and listened to every young person who would talk to me.

It became clear as I listened to the kids that in their minds this summer camp had nothing to do with cancer. It had to do with having fun. They talked about their pets, their baseball card collections, beanie babies, swimming, vacations with their families, even school. The girls talked about boys. The boys talked about girls. They both talked about the Friday night dance.

Since most of the kids at Camp Goodtimes are cancer patients, they play and laugh and swim and sail and eat and sleep with one common and constant companion. Their cancer is with them day and night. But it doesn't stop them from having fun. They deal with it.

Their cancer is with them day and night. But it doesn't stop them from having fun. They deal with it.

Some line up at the nurse's station once or twice a day for their medication. Some choose to sit quietly when they feel tired. The teenagers handle it by talking about it with other teens who become close friends during their week at the camp.

Since that first year, I've gone back for short visits every June. Every year I see faces I remember, but every year there are faces I don't see. That's the reality of cancer. It takes young lives.

Every year on the first night of camp the counselors meet for what they call the "memory circle." They remember and talk about campers who died during the past year.

* * * * * *

"Some years are better than others," a staffer told me this past June. "Last year no one was in the memory circle. This year five of the kids are being remembered." There's no dwelling on the subject, just the sharing of sweet memories about the kids who are gone.

As I pull away from the campsite every summer, I thank God for the volunteers and donors who make this wonderful week possible for the kids. I pray that someday we will find a cure for cancer, but until that day I'm grateful that kids fighting cancer can share smiles and fun at a special place called Camp Goodtimes.

Focus Your Light

The lesson I learn from the kids at Camp Goodtimes is that the human spirit is tougher than any disease. Courage is written on the faces of every young person I've ever met there. Find a "Camp Goodtimes" in your area. Become a volunteer. If time is an issue, make a cash donation. It will be appreciated.

*   *   *   *   *   *

Chapter Twenty-four
THANK GOD WE'RE LATE

I know that every good and excellent thing in the world stands moment by moment on the razor-edge of danger and must be fought for. . . .

—Thornton Wilder

In the winter of 2001-2002 I was asked to make a short presentation at an event called "Un-Sung Heroes Night" at Skyline High School in Sammamish. That night I met a young woman named Danielle and her mom, Nancy. Immediately I could tell they were part of a very intelligent, enthusiastic family.

A week or so after that meeting Nancy called to tell me that Danielle would be going to Israel for the last quarter of her junior year. She would be studying at the Alexander Muss High School in Hod Ha'Sharon, about 20 miles north of Tel Aviv.

In light of the September 11th terrorist attacks and all the trouble in the Middle East, my first reaction was fear. I pictured myself going and wondered how this young person living in a safe environment would deal with a summer in Israel. Now I know.

In mid-July—just three days after her return home—I waited for Danielle at a local coffee shop. Through the window I could see her bounding from her yellow Volkswagen Rabbit toward the door. Her blue eyes were bright in her suntanned face.

"My outlook on life has changed," Danielle said with an energy and enthusiasm that caused anyone nearby to want to listen. "While I was there I tried to talk and listen to everyone around. It was incredible!

Everywhere I went the people welcomed me with open arms. It was wonderful!"

On April 21, 2002, Danielle and twenty-two other young men and women from across America left home on long flights to Tel Aviv and a spring they would never forget. "We took regular classes at the school three times a week, then the other three days a week we'd go on field trips to actually see what we had discussed the previous day."

Danielle's favorite teacher was a man named Ruvin Spiro. He had taught in the Midwest in the United States, then became a Hasidic Jew, moved to Israel, and began teaching at the Alexander Muss High School.

"He has such passion for teaching, "said Danielle. "He told of unconditional friendship and love among families and communities throughout Israel. And he was so much fun to learn from because he enjoyed teaching so much."

Danielle told me about her short stay at a youth hostel in Tiberius and her conversation with an 18-year-old Arab man. "We got along great and talked all day and night about issues between Arabs and Jews. We had a great conversation. But even with our friendly discussion and debate, we couldn't come up with a solution for the problems in the Middle East."

"The young people of Israel have a desire to serve their country, travel, experience life. It's not all about going to a fun college then making lots of money. People are really grateful just to be alive."

Then there was the story of the scary train ride even her mother didn't know about. "We were on a train ride and somewhere down the line a bomb blew up the tracks," Danielle told me. "An Israeli soldier sitting near me on the train said quietly, 'Thank God we're late or we might have been there when the bomb went off.'"

Danielle paused briefly, then continued. "They have a program in Israel for older people called Life Line. It's a place where older citizens can come and use their skills, get paid, and sell their products

* * * * * *

in a market. It's such a productive way to spend one's later years.

"Every young person serves their country in some form of national service. The boys go to the military for three years, the girls for two. By the time young people are 18 years old, they're grown up. They've learned so much about life, it's amazing."

Danielle paused again, then added, "The young people of Israel have a desire to serve their country, travel, experience life. It's not all about going to a fun college then making lots of money. People are really grateful just to be alive."

As our conversation sped into its second hour, Danielle told of helping a Russian woman on her flight back to the United States. "She wanted to go to Los Angeles and couldn't speak any English. We landed at JFK in New York and I couldn't leave her. I helped her find someone who would show her where to get the flight to Los Angeles."

Danielle, her friend Elise from Eastlake High School, Samara from Mercer Island High School, and twenty other young men and women chose to experience something most others would not do. As a result of their decision to set aside fear and anxiety in favor of the celebration of the human spirit, they spent a month none of them will ever forget.

Focus Your Light

Become more aware of the world. Not just your world, but the larger circle that includes all mankind. Do something you're afraid of doing. Go somewhere new. Reach out to someone outside your circle of friends. Seek to understand before being understood.

Chapter Twenty-five
FISHING FOR A NEW IDEA

The secret to success in life is to make your vocation your vacation.

—Mark Twain

I have a brother-in-law named Earl. Not a big deal, I know. According to a recent study by the American Census Bureau, everyone has a brother-in-law named Earl. But my brother-in-law is special. He's an inventor.

Earl was born in Bridgeport, Connecticut, on a cold winter day in 1941. He grew up in a large family, went to public schools, and graduated from Harding High in 1959. That fall Earl was off to the University of Connecticut to study engineering, where he met my sister. Five years later they were married and I joined the millions of Americans who are related to someone named Earl.

Earl and my sister left the East Coast for Seattle in the mid-sixties when he landed a job at Boeing. The job was fine, but Earl and Mary Jane missed Connecticut and their families and within months were back on the East Coast. They've been there ever since.

Earl settled into a good engineering job at a large Connecticut company and worked there for several years. He was a good employee, well liked, and probably would have stayed there until retirement. But, unfortunately, things began to change. Earl sensed that his services would no longer be needed by the company, so in the mid-1990s he began to look for another means of income.

Keep in mind that this is a guy who did the plumbing and some of the electrical wiring in his own house. He's also a very good basketball player and an avid fly fisherman.

Also keep in mind the number of times you've heard a friend say, "If only I could make a living doing something I love, I'd be happy." Well, Earl is a quiet guy, so you wouldn't hear him say that out loud, but I know that's what he was thinking.

He eliminated basketball immediately. There's not much call for a 50-something white guy, no matter what kind of jump shot he has. Earl may have considered plumbing briefly but quickly shelved that idea too. And that left fly-fishing, which is where the story really gets going.

After working for years on his fly-casting skills, Earl determined that the vibration of the handle and the tip of the rod kept the line from being cast as far as it could be. The result of months of research was a much-improved fly rod, now sold worldwide.

Most people would have left the project alone after that first level of success, but not Earl. He still wasn't satisfied with the length of his casts. His work continued well into the cold, snowy winter of 1997.

Working in his unheated garage twelve hours a day, Earl devised a new plan, a better fly line, one that would travel fifteen to twenty feet farther than anything else on the market. Using heating elements from old toaster ovens supplemented with charcoal briquettes from his patio grill, Earl devised a way to bake on a new friction-free coating that would revolutionize fly lines everywhere.

In that chilly garage in the company of lawn mowers and snow blowers, old boots, fishing waders, deflated basketballs, and odd pieces of lumber left behind from outdoor projects, the new fly line was born.

This quiet man sneaking up on 60 years of age has achieved the dream of most people who get up and go to work every day—the dream of taking something they love and creating a living out of it. Earl hasn't just invented two new fishing products sold worldwide. He's reinvented himself.

* * * * * *

Bright Idea
Be Creative

A. Gather one or two special friends who are not afraid to dream.

B. Give each friend a notebook and a pen.

C. Now start brain storming new ideas, new concepts, "out of the box" methods for finding success.

D. Write down a hundred ideas among all of you. Make them wild and crazy. When you reach one hundred pick the top ten and start the process all over again.

E. By the end of the evening you'll be amazed at how excited you are, how free you feel, and what great ideas you came up with.

F. Narrow the ideas down to five, then three, then one. Get energy from each other and the ideas will flow. Who knows, you might even quit your job tomorrow!

* * * * * *

Chapter Twenty-six

THE LAST LAUGH

The most wasted day is that in which we have not laughed.

—Sebastian R. N. Chamfort

Late at night on October 1, 1998 I was lying in bed reading and I remember turning to my wife Mika and saying something like, "Gee, I wish I didn't have to fly to Connecticut tomorrow. I'm so beat from work. I'd like to put it off for a month or so."

Mika smiled and said, "You can't put it off. You're going to go, and I'm going with you."

The next night we sat with my mom and dad at their kitchen table and listened to stories about their first date, their wedding and the early years of their lives together. Even though both were in their mid-80's and a bit prone to short-term memory lapses, their stories of the early years were crisp, enthusiastic and accurate.

As we took the flight back home a few days later, I was glad we'd made the trip and looked forward to more stories at Thanksgiving.

Two weeks later Dad died.

I thank my wife every day for making me take that early October trip and allowing me a final opportunity to hear my father tell his fascinating stories.

———◆———

October 22, 1998, was a day I thought we could put off forever, but we couldn't. On that sunny, cool, crisp, delightful New England afternoon we would lay my father to rest in Hillside Cemetery in Wilton, Connecticut.

It was just three days earlier that my dad's neighbor and nurse, Susan, had called in tears to inform me that Dad had collapsed mowing the lawn and medics had rushed him to the hospital.

Only an hour later my nephew, Tony, phoned to say my dad, his grandpa, had passed away a few moments earlier.

Then minutes later my cousin, Scott, whom Dad had taken under his wing when his own father died six years earlier, called. "I just wanted to make sure you knew and, Tony, it's a beautiful day here, your dad's favorite kind of day."

My sense of duty to my mother and the rest of the family held me together, as I called the travel agent to book a flight to Connecticut, then called my children to let them know their grandpa had died.

Later that day we all laughed out loud at the small numbers written on the outside frame of the garage door. My dad had written "C345," the code for the garage door opener. He never worried about break-ins, but he wanted to make sure any of us could get into the garage in case he wasn't home.

Tears came on and off that day, but I was comforted by one thing. I knew that, despite the sad duties that lay ahead in the next 72 hours, laughter would again ring through my parents' house. That was my father's way, and it would still be that way in his absence.

I was right about the first part. Tears flowed again when I saw my mom, my sister Mary Jane, my brother Phil, his wife Fran and my niece Linda, all of whom had taken such good care of my dad in his final years.

As I walked through Dad's garden only 24 hours after I got the phone call, a smile came back to my face. I saw the crude fencing he had built so many years ago to keep the deer and rabbits out.

* * * * * *

There was the pan and the hose where he washed the lettuce before bringing it into the house. And way back on the two-acre property was the shed. We always had an old shed when I was growing up. This latest shed had two old ride-on mowers, a snow blower, several ancient farm tools and a couple of bags of rock salt for the driveway in winter.

I smile into the mirror first thing in the morning and do the same thing at night. I look at myself, and say, "Okay Tony, you had a pretty good day, get some quality sleep and give it your best shot again tomorrow. Now let me see that smile. Good. Now go to bed."

The shed brought another smile to my face. So did the old dog kennel, the clothesline, a telephone rigged on the wall of the garage only four feet high so my mother could reach it and two bags filled with old barber tools.

Later that day we all laughed out loud at the small numbers written on the outside frame of the garage door. My dad had written "C345," the code for the garage door opener. He never worried about break-ins, but he wanted to make sure any of us could get into the garage in case he wasn't home.

Well, he wasn't home now and he wouldn't be anymore, but we were laughing again, convinced that Dad was laughing along with us. He taught us all to smile and laugh and we weren't about to forget that lesson.

Now, three years later, my routine remains the same, but I've added to it. I smile into the mirror first thing in the morning and do the same thing at night. I look at myself, and say, "Okay, Tony, you had a pretty good day, get some quality sleep and give it your best shot again tomorrow. Now let me see that smile. Good. Now go to bed."

* * * * *

Focus Your Light

Is there someone close to you who needs a phone call or a visit from you? How often do you postpone that trip to see your parents because you're tired, watching the game, low on cash or too busy?

Now is the time to hear your mom talk about her childhood. Now is the time to let Dad ramble on about his time in the army. Now is the time to visit Grandpa and Grandma. Now is the time to call your aunt in Albany. And while you're on the phone ask about my aunt in Utica will you?

All during his life my dad gave to others. He didn't give much in the way of material items. He gave his time, his humor, his labor and his love. He mowed the lawn of his elderly next door neighbor when she was recovering from cancer. He dug a new garden for his young neighbors across the street. In fact, there stands in that spot a memorial garden in my father's name.

My dad grew tomatoes and gave them away all over the neighborhood. I was with him one time when he visited an old hunting buddy in Vermont and he made a stop at a Dairy Queen to get a cup of soft ice cream because it was his friend's favorite and he knew the old guy couldn't drive anymore.

"Late in life," my dad used to say, "it's not money that's important, it's not any possession; it's friends and family and good times and laughter."

I smile every time I picture him saying that.

* * * * * *

CONCLUSION

My son Pete called the other day. He needed a haircut. He didn't have time to get away from the auto dealership where he was working, so he asked if I'd come over the cut his hair.

I love the opportunity to cut hair. I don't get to do it much anymore. So I drove to the dealership, set up my traveling shop and gave him my famous "close on the sides, a little off the top" special.

As I was cutting Pete's hair I thought of my dad and the struggle he had teaching me how to become a barber. I remembered the tough time he had teaching a left-handed son to work with right-handed tools, but I eventually learned and became quite good at it.

The same was true of all the jobs I took on after that. Difficult at first, easier by the day, then enjoyable and satisfying.

I'm at a point in my life now where I'm always looking for new challenges. I've studied politics all my life and have a rich curiosity about that field. It's not much different from being a sportscaster or a barber for that matter. You meet people, listen to their points of view, form your own opinion and proceed from there.

It might even be possible to tie all of my former careers into a new career in politics. I can pick up votes by talking to people about sports, and if they still won't vote for me I can offer them a cookie recipe, jelly donuts the size of softballs or a free haircut.

Life is a wonderful adventure, especially when you open your eyes and see the magic of every day. You can decide what this day will bring like no one else can. If you're on your way to work, be grateful you have a job. If you're on your way to school, be grateful you're going to know something tonight you didn't know this morning.

Life is a wonderful adventure, especially when you open your eyes and see the magic of every day.

If it's a sunny day, you're happy because you love sunny days. If it's raining, you don't have to water the lawn and your duck friends are happy.

If the stock market is soaring you can be grateful you bought low. If the market is falling you can look forward to buying low. It's all about attitude. You are in control of your life from this moment on. You will get what you want because no one can stop you without your permission.

Cherish your friends, your memories, your family and yourself. Life is a wonderful treasure and there's plenty for everyone.

* * * * *

Imagine.